BRIEF APOLOGIA FOR
THE CHURCH OF THE AGES

"Among the heroes of orthodoxy who arose during and after Vatican II towered Fr. Roger-Thomas Calmel, who, with the strength born of a rigorous Thomism, identified, critiqued, and warned against the errors and sacrileges of his time. And now that Catholics who were young and foolish at the time of the Council are wreaking new havoc as old and foolish princes of the Church, Calmel's *Brief Apologia*, his most characteristic, poignant, and incisive work, suddenly shines with renewed relevance. We may rejoice that this superlative classic of Catholic traditionalist thought is available, at last, in English!"

—DR. PETER KWASNIEWSKI, author of *The Once and Future Roman Rite*

Brief *Apologia*
for the
CHURCH OF THE AGES

ROGER-THOMAS CALMEL, O.P.

Foreword by Fr Thomas Crean, O.P.
Postface by Jean Madiran
Translated by Gerhard Eger

AROUCA
PRESS

Taken from the 2017 edition of *Brève apologie pour l'Église de toujours* published by Dominique Martin Morin (Poitiers, France), 2017.

Waterloo, N2J 0A5
www.aroucapress.com

ISBN: 978-1-998492-70-1

CONTENTS

TRANSLATORS' NOTE

FATHER ROGER-THOMAS CALMEL'S *Brief Apologia for the Church of the Ages* was written between late 1970 and early 1971. Its chapters were first published as successive articles in the journal *Itinéraires* from March to July 1971, then compiled as a separate booklet in the autumn. In 2017, the Teaching Dominican Sisters of the Holy Name of Jesus and the Immaculate Heart of Mary in Brignoles (Var) published a third edition, adding a new chapter, "Authority and Holiness in the Church," as intended by the author, along with corrections he had prepared for a potential reprint. They also included six appendices composed of other articles by Father Calmel that clarify, complement, or expand on points in the *Brief Apologia*.

This first English translation follows that third edition. Where possible, translations of the works cited by Father Calmel have been provided in the citations. Translations of Holy Scripture are taken from the revised Douay-Rheims version, except where Father Calmel himself has paraphrased the text. Italics are the author's own.

May this translation serve to introduce Anglophone readers to a vital voice in the defense of Catholic Tradition, one whose insights and counsel remain as pertinent today as they were when they were first written, mired as we remain in the crisis unleashed by the Second Vatican Council, a crisis Father Calmel was one of the first to recognize and confront.

The translator
Octave of the Assumption of
the Blessed Virgin Mary
2025

ROGER CALMEL WAS BORN INTO a deeply Catholic family in south-west France, just before the outbreak of the Great War. He was educated first in a minor, then in a major, seminary, but desiring something other than the life of a parish priest, he entered the Order of Preachers in 1936, adding the religious name "Thomas" to that of his baptism. Ordained in 1941, he worked at first in Toulouse and Marseille, preaching in schools and parishes, assisting with retreats and pilgrimages and with the journals of the Dominican friars. After the end of the Second World War, he gave much help to the Dominican teaching sisters of the Holy Name of Jesus, not least with the reform of their Constitutions. Yet especially from the middle of the 1950's, he found himself on the margins of ecclesial life, as the Church in France fell increasingly under the spell of Marxism and of the ideas, if so they may be called, of Pierre Teilhard de Chardin.

Even before the Second Vatican Council, Father Calmel warned in many books and articles of the coming storm, and once the council had finished, he was among those who refused to speak of renewal when they could see collapse. In November 1969, three days before the *Novus Ordo Missæ* of Pope Paul VI began to be celebrated throughout the Latin church, he wrote a public declaration explaining why he felt bound rather to continue with the rite of his ordination. His friends and admirers feared that the declaration would be censured by Rome, but as he had predicted, it was ignored.

In his remaining years, he continued to write, to encourage the faithful and especially to assist those Dominican teaching sisters who wished to retain their liturgy, habit and constitutions. With the permission of his superiors, he spent the last months of his life in Brignoles, which would become the mother house of a flourishing family of schools. He died there on the old feast of the finding of the Cross, 3 May 1975, at the age of sixty.

What is the literary genre of the present work? It is not a treatise on ecclesiology or on any other branch of theology, even though the author was at home in them all, having been formed in the school of St Thomas Aquinas, in the great Dominican convent of St Maximin in Provence. Nor is it, like the *Apologia* of Newman, a work of autobiography, even though here and there one catches glimpses of Father Calmel's own travails and combats. Nor is it exactly a work of spirituality, a book written primarily to promote devotion, even though whoever reads it in a spirit of faith can hope to receive a renewed sense of spiritual realities and of the beauty of the Catholic creed.

Rather, it is a work of prophecy. Like Jeremiah or Ezekiel under the Old Law, Roger-Thomas Calmel spoke and wrote as a priest who suffered to see God dishonoured and His people led astray. Those ancient prophets were charged by God to speak against false doctrine; to warn the people of God and their leaders to return to the fear of the Lord, in their worship and in their daily lives; and thus to prevent Israel from being dissolved into the nations round about. Father Calmel, simple priest of the New Law, likewise spoke out against what his sometime mentor, Jacques Maritain, had called "immanent apostasy": the widespread dissolution, within the visible Church, of dogma, and the replacement of supernatural faith, hope, and charity by merely human simulacra.

To Jeremiah, God said: *I have made thee a wall of brass to the kings of Juda, to the princes thereof, and to the priests, and to the people of the land* (Jer. 1:18). To Ezekiel: *I have made thy face like adamant and like flint* (Ez. 3:9). Father Calmel seems to have received some portion of their spirit: like them, he took up the burden of a message that he knew would be unwelcome. *Whether they hear or whether they forbear, they will know that a prophet has been among them* (Ez. 2:5). His *Apologia* is a book written without fear.

Does that make him a harsh or unsympathetic figure? No more than those ancient seers are rendered inhuman in our eyes by the severity of their message. What distinguishes the present work from many other critiques of "post-conciliar neo-modernism" is that we feel throughout that the author's intransigence is motivated by an ardent love: love of Jesus Christ, of His Church, and of His words. Like the old prophets, he had tasted the scroll of God that is *sweet as honey in the mouth* (Ez. 3:3). How else could he have continued, when he experienced the rejection that is the prophet's common lot?

Of course, as St Thomas Aquinas remarks following St Gregory the Great, even a true prophet may sometimes err, by not fully distinguishing what comes from his own spirit and what comes from the Spirit of God.[1] The reader must judge for himself to what extent Father Calmel's warnings and denunciations were well founded. Or perhaps it is still too soon to be sure.[2] For, half a century

---

[1] *Summa theologiæ* IIa-IIae q. 171, a. 5. This qualification does not of course apply to the prophetical books in the Bible, since all that is asserted by the scriptural authors is asserted by the Holy Spirit.
[2] There is however one question where I should give my opinion, seeing the importance of what it at stake. I think that he was incorrect to suppose that an eclipse or a loss of supernatural faith on the part of many bishops was liable so to change their sacramental

after his death, the Church still resembles that 'sea-battle by night' to which St Basil the Great compared the crisis of his own time. Into this persisting darkness, the words of Roger-Thomas Calmel still shine a penetrating light.

Fr Thomas Crean, O. P.
November 12, 2025

---

intention as to render their sacraments doubtful or invalid. The analogy with the Edwardine bishops of 16th century England is imperfect, since these did not confer their later sacraments as bishops of the Catholic Church, and as thus publicly committed to her sacramental intention.

PROLOGUE

DECEIVED BY THE GRAND CHImera of discovering the certain and facile means to secure, once and for all, universal religious unity, certain prelates—even those in the highest positions—are striving to fashion a Church without borders, where all men, dispensed from renouncing the world and Satan, might soon gather in liberty and fraternity. Dogmas, rites, hierarchy, and even asceticism, should one insist, may persist from the original Church, but they are to be stripped of the safeguards Our Lord willed and Tradition refined. As a result, everything is to be emptied of its Catholic vigour, that is, of grace and sanctity. Adherents of the most disparate beliefs, and even those who reject all belief, shall then find easy entry into the Church, or rather, the mirage of a Church. This is the current project of the eminent Master of lies and illusions. This is the grand design of Masonic inspiration that he drives his minions to undertake: priests bereft of faith promoted to become prestigious theologians together with bishops who are oblivious, treacherous, or even covert apostates, swiftly raised to the pinnacle of honour and entrusted with the highest prelatures. They squander their lives and forfeit their souls constructing a *post-Conciliar Church, under the sun of Satan.*[1]

Dogmas, increasingly undermined by the relativism of the new *pastoral approach* that condemns no heresy, no longer convey a clear and supernatural truth. As a result, it is no longer necessary to incline one's understanding or purify one's heart to receive them, assuming the word still has a meaning in this case. The sacraments are now accessible to those who do not believe. Hardly anything

---

[1] A reference to Georges Bernanos's novel *Under the Sun of Satan.*

prevents unbelievers or the unworthy from partaking in them, so estranged have the new *ecclesiastical rites* become, through their instability and fluidity, from the *sacramental sign* that is *efficacious in itself* and divinely established by our Saviour once and for all *until His return.*

As for the hierarchy, it is gradually dissolving into *the people of God,* of which it is becoming a democratic emanation, elected by universal suffrage for temporary functions. Thanks to these unprecedented innovations, churchmen take pride in having torn down the barriers that, in the not-so-distant pre-Conciliar era, kept out those who rejected dogmas, spurned the sacraments, and refused to submit to the hierarchy. Indeed, as understood before the Council, dogmas, sacraments, governance, and the requirement of interior conversion gave the Church the semblance of a fortified city — *Jerusalem quæ* ædificatur *ut civitas*[2] — with well-guarded gates and impregnable ramparts. No one could cross the divine threshold without first having converted. Today, however, everything is changing before our eyes. Beliefs, rites, and the interior life are undergoing a process of universal dissolution so extreme and refined that one can no longer distinguish between Catholics and non-Catholics. It is now *outdated* to give yes-or-no answers and definitions and consider them as definitive, and so one wonders what could possibly prevent even non-Christian religions from joining the new *universal* Church, continually updated through ecumenical considerations.

If one accepts the point of view so many Fathers ensnared by Vatican II allowed to be imposed upon them, it is necessary to devise a completely novel system and an unprecedented framework in order to win the world over to the Church without risking failure or suffering

---

[2] Psalm 121, *Lætatus sum in his quæ dicta sunt mihi.*

persecution, beginning by relativizing the supernatural. But this is pointless. For, on the one hand, Jesus said, "The servant is not greater than his lord. If they have persecuted me, they will also persecute you: if they have kept my word, they will keep yours also."[3] On the other hand, the supernatural cannot be altered or diminished. It is firm and precise, possessing an established nature and a clear and definitive form. Since the Incarnation of the Word, our redemption through the Cross, and the descent of the Holy Ghost, the supernatural is exclusively Christian and Catholic. It exists solely *in Christo Jesu, et Virgine Maria et Ecclesia Christi*. This is why, if one holds in one's soul the truth of Jesus Christ's Gospel and the first twenty councils, one clearly sees what forces the chimera of ecumenical unity into nothingness: the duty to bend the knee before the Son of man, sovereign author and dispenser of Salvation, solely within the one Church He established.

Too many high-ranking churchmen have surrendered themselves to the modernist corruption of the intellect. They have come to the point where it no longer strikes them as monstrous to assert, in a single speech, propositions that are mutually incompatible, because they consider the intellect incapable of truth. They suppose instead that somewhere—no one quite knows where—there exists a sort of religious *noumenon*, elusive and unreachable, about which the mind constructs clever systems, endlessly variable according to the evolution of our species, but always incapable of attaining what is. To them, one thing alone matters: that these systems, ideologies, and theologies serve the advancement of mankind. Their worth is judged by their power to inspire a great upward march toward liberty and progress.

---

[3] John 15:20.

Those who consent to such a spiritual distortion refuse to condemn either heresies or heretics, and do not consider themselves bound by any dogma. They view even the most contradictory theses with detachment and benevolence, striving to find in each whatever elements might contribute to a better future and that are closely or remotely linked to a so-called spirit of the Gospel. But they see the Gospel not as a definitive rule preserved by divinely assisted Tradition, but as a ferment of some ideal future yet to come. When prelates with such warped minds occupy the highest positions in the Church, it is an unspeakable affliction for all the faithful. "If that time were not to be cut short, not a soul would be saved; but that time will be cut short, for the sake of those whom God has chosen."[4]

Driven by seemingly noble motives to covet with all their strength and from their very first steps in the clerical state the highest offices in the Church, young priests have offered the devil an all too easy prey. He has taken them under his wing to bring them to those exalted ranks, exacting a ruinous toll. During the mediaeval or classical ages of Christendom, anyone seeking advancement to the cardinalate or an even loftier station often had to become complicit, at least by his silence, in the sins and misdeeds of Christian princes. Today, Christian princes no longer exist; at any rate, they have been dispossessed. Power has passed into the hands of secret societies, whether Masonic or communist. These, to a large extent, are the dreadful masters of the modern age.

Therefore, a priest who aspires to rise to the Church's highest ranks today must reckon with these princes. He must become complicit with them. Can he rise without consenting—perhaps gradually, but truly—to a radical

---

[4] Matthew 24:22

corruption of the spirit? For if he resisted being slowly engulfed by spiritual darkness, he would be incapable, despite his efforts, of serving as a useful instrument for the forces of evil. One way or another, he would stand athwart them; he would remain their adversary. Yet he must help them; it is for no other purpose that the modern Caesar has raised him to positions of authority.

Sometimes a man or a woman, drunk with passion, willingly and with chilling resolve surrenders their sacred freedom to the demon of lust. The demon, claiming mastery, thus seems invested with the power to drag them into the abyss, nearly paralyzing their will. Yet the demon of pride poses a far greater threat than that of carnal desire. Consider, then, the fearsome hold of this demon over a priest who, greedy for power in spiritual matters, aligns himself—however indirectly—with the occult powers of our age, over which the demon reigns as lord. To what depths of delusion will the demon not drag this ambitious priest? If he does not recover himself in time, his reason will be invincibly warped, as it were, by the Prince of this world.

> On the pillow of evil, it is Satan Trismegistus
> Who shall *soon lull his* enchanted mind,
> *And the priceless metal of all loyalty*
> *Shall* be vaporized by this learned alchemist.[5]

But even if the Church's distress were a hundred times more heart-rending, a hundred times more cruel, the Lord is and remains forever her Master and her King. To Him "has been given all power; before Him every knee bends, in heaven, on earth, and in hell,"[6] including in that pecu-

---

[5] Translator's note: A quotation, with amendments in italics, from the first poem in Charles Baudelaire's *Fleurs du mal.*
[6] Matthew 28:18 and Philippians 2:9–10.

liar, momentarily painless hell that is the modernist sect. It cannot extend its harmful influence beyond the narrow boundaries Our Lord assigns to it. Our Lord does grant it a certain power to obscure, distort, and scandalize in myriad ways, but only for the good of the elect and to increase the splendour of grace in His Church. We must not fear, therefore, but rather confidently persevere in the Church of the ages.

Brief *Apologia*
for the
CHURCH OF THE AGES

Two Inseparable Aspects of the Mystery of the Church

T HE CHURCH IS, INDIVISIBLY, both the *mediatrix of salvation* through her preaching, sacraments, and hierarchy, and the *sacred dwelling wherein God abides*, both through the charity that ever burns in her heart and through the Eucharistic presence of the Lord Jesus, who nourishes that charity. The Church exercises her mediating function only during her pilgrimage *through this vale of tears*, but she is the tabernacle of God both during the time of combat in exile and during her ineffable repose in the eternal fatherland. For she is aflame with the same love on earth as in paradise, but in heaven that love proceeds from the vision, whereas on earth it springs from faith and the sacraments of faith.

The Church could not fulfil her mediating function without certain conditions. If they were lacking, it would indeed be impossible for her to dispense grace with certainty, to proclaim the truth without alteration, or to celebrate worship through a liturgy faithful and pleasing to the Heavenly Father. Moreover, should this mediating function cease, the Church would also cease to be the dwelling-place of God among men. For how could the Lord continue to reside under the Eucharistic species if the dogmas of faith, valid ordinations, and the modest yet exacting laws governing sacramental celebrations by which this presence becomes effective were no longer guaranteed? And how could the dogmas of faith, valid ordinations, and the modest yet exacting laws of the holy Mass remain secure and retain their validity if the rites were no longer subject to precise regulation? If dogmatic formulas and the power of holy orders were disregarded? If formularies and rites were abandoned to the whims of the celebrant and the vagaries of the assembly?

If these modest conditions for the real Eucharistic presence were destroyed, the Church would perish. For if the Eucharistic presence ceased, how would theological charity be nourished and sustained? And if divine charity were not supported and fed, how could it endure? From the moment this charity should fade, the Church would no longer deserve her supreme title: *the tabernacle of God among men.*[1] She would cease to exist.

Thus the dignity of the Church—which is twofold, as dispenser of grace and dwelling-place of God—is kept alive and shines forth because certain conditions are observed. It is one of the modernists' deceptions to speak of the Church in every conceivable way, while working with scientific precision to strip her of the means to live, whether by relativizing the definitions of the faith, dismantling the rites, or making up some naturalistic reinterpretation of

---

[1] Review the entirety of chapter 21 of the Apocalypse and the hymns for the feast of the Dedication (the Dominican rite preserves them in their original form). See also the admirable work of Father Humbert Clérissac, O. P., *The Mystery of the Church* (London: Sheed & Ward, 1937).

supernatural charity. As if the Church could preserve the faith, spread it throughout the world, and nourish her children with the truths of salvation, yet disregard—when she must proclaim "words that shall never pass away"[2]—the formal terms and irreformable dogmas guarded by anathemas. As if the Church could be alive with grace and communicate it to us, yet quietly allow the breakdown of her own rites, even though she herself established them to protect and solemnize the sacramental signs that confer grace. As if the Church could remain steadfast and unshaken as the supernatural, hierarchical society of Christ's grace, while allowing the personal form of government with which the Lord endowed her, and the primacy of Peter given as her foundation, to be utterly overturned under the insidious attacks of democratic *collegiality*.

The numerous and coordinated modernist attacks directed at demolishing what some call *the juridical apparatus* of the Church do not greatly surprise us. After all, "the disciple is not above the master,"[3] nor is the Bride greater than the Bridegroom. Yet these attacks do not alarm us, because we are assured that the Church shall overcome them. The Church is not a man-made institution; *she comes from heaven, from God Himself.* She is "the tabernacle of God among men."[4] Thus, by both her origin and her nature, she stands apart from all earthly institutions, however noble or admirable they may be, which must sooner or later succumb to defeat, sometimes irreparably.

Just as one cannot say that Christ on the Cross was defeated—since His power and love turned that most bitter suffering into a sacrifice of infinite worth, wholly pleasing to the Father and entirely effective for the redemption

---

[2] Matthew 24:35.
[3] John 13:16.
[4] Apocalypse 21:3.

of mankind—so too one cannot say that the Church, even
when persecuted from without and betrayed from within,
is defeated or doomed to perish. On the contrary, her
divine power and sanctity remain ever strong and active
enough that even in the midst of iniquity, charity abounds.
The Church is victorious because she is the Bride of the
victorious Christ. The Church is invincible, although her
children may suffer defeat and often fall. Yet so long as
they remain within her bosom, their defeat is never final.
When they are overcome, it is because they have separated themselves from her. But even then, they cannot
strip her of the strength that has been given to her forever:
the power to draw them back and to sanctify them. Both
before and after their defection, she remains the unfailing
dispenser of salvation and the holy temple of God. Those
who abandon her are lost, but she herself is never lost.
Because conquering is an inalienable prerogative of the
Lord Jesus Christ,[5] it is, by necessity, a prerogative of His
Bride as well. *Vicit leo de tribu Juda.*[6]

As the Church is engulfed by the rolling mists and
smoke of infernal modernism, to profess the faith of the
Church in her dogmas and sacraments is *to preserve intact*
her traditional definitions and rites. These are honest, clear,
and free from all ambiguity. To confess the faith of the
Church in the face of modernism, to rejoice in the privilege of suffering in order to bear noble witness to a Church
betrayed on every side, is to watch with her in her agony,
or to watch with Jesus Himself, who continues the agony
He once endured in the Garden of Olives in His afflicted

---

[5] On this point, far too often forgotten, concerning the inevitable
victory of Christ, we would refer the reader to our earlier brief treatise, *Théologie de l'Histoire*, chapter 2, "Lumière de l'Apocalypse,"
at the end of the chapter, pp. 50ff.

[6] "The Lion of the tribe of Juda hath prevailed" (Apocalypse 5:5).

and betrayed Bride. Insofar as we remain faithful watchmen, untouched by worldly fear or by discouragement, we shall come to know by experience that Holy Church is a mystery of supernatural strength and divine peace: *Urbs Jerusalem beata, dicta pacis visio.*[7]

Blessed city of Jerusalem,	*Urbs Jerusalem beata*
Called the vision of peace	*Dicta pacis visio*
Which is built in heaven	*Quæ construitur in cælis*
Out of living stones	*Vivis ex lapidibus*
For whom the angels make a crown	*Et Angelis coronata*
As for a bride her maids of honour.	*Ut sponsata comite.*

New and come from heaven,	*Nova veniens e cælo*
For the intimacy of the nuptials,	*Nuptiali thalamo,*
Prepared like a Bride,	*Præparata ut sponsata*
May she be united to the Lord.	*Copuletur Domino.*
Her courts and her ramparts	*Plateæ et muri ejus*
Are entirely of pure gold.	*Ex auro purissimo.*

Gleaming with precious stones, the doors	*Portæ nitent margaritis*
	Adytis patentibus,
Are open onto the sanctuary,	*Et virtute meritorum*
And by virtue of his merits,	*Illuc introducitur*
Thither penetrates	*Omnis qui hoc Christi*
He who for Christ's name	*nomen*
Bears suffering here below.	*Hic in mundo premitur.*

Cut with great strokes by the chisel,	*Tunsionibus pressuris*
And polished to perfection, the beautiful stones	*Expoliti lapides*
	Suis coaptatur locis
Are placed each in their place	*Per manu Artificis.*
By the hand of the master builder.	*Disponuntur permansuri*
They are arranged to remain without end	*Sacris ædificiis.*
In the edifice of all holiness.	

---

[7] We here provide the original version of this hymn, prior to the infelicitous alterations made at the beginning of the seventeenth century. The Dominican Breviary, like those of other proper uses, has preserved it free from any alterations or revisions.

Urbs Jerusalem: not *platea*, a public square, a mere gathering-place for chatterers, demagogues, and false preachers of a new religion; not a fairground, a thoroughfare for tourists, swindlers and mountebanks; but a true and noble city, *urbs*, inhabited by worthy subjects, a stronghold fortified with towers and ramparts, governed by a head and a hierarchy, a city whose common good is revealed doctrine faithfully transmitted, the seven sacraments with the Blessed Sacraments above all, and the charity of the saints—the city of the eight evangelical beatitudes. *Urbs Jerusalem beata.*

Dicta pacis visio: pacis visio quia reconciliationis visio. A city of peace because it is the city of reconciliation with God through the Blood of His Only-Begotten Son Jesus Christ. This Blood was shed for once and for all on Calvary as the price of our redemption, but the real offering is *efficaciously* commemorated each day upon our altars under the Eucharistic species, until the Lord returns. By the sacrifice of the Mass, sins are forgiven, conflicts overcome, and the greatest sufferings soothed. God is adored, thanked, and imported according to a worship worthy of Him. Through the power of the Holy Sacrifice, offered *in truth according to the rite of the ages*, the holy city's days are ordered in peace:[8] *dicta pacis visio.*

This goodly city, impregnable and blessed, this city of peace, which through preaching and holy baptism unceasingly grows with new subjects, knows no origin outside the celestial, for its very essence is supernatural. *This Kingdom is not of this world.*

Nova veniens e cælo. The holy city is "come from heaven." It proceeds from Christ's open Heart and from

---

[8] See in the *Hanc igitur oblationem* during the prayers before the Consecration: *diesque nostros* in tua pace *disponas.*

the sacraments that thence flow forth and bestow upon every generation the graces of His redemptive Passion. This true Church proceeds from the Holy Ghost, whom Jesus, having ascended to God's right hand, sent upon her on the day of Pentecost, and continues to send, not to found her anew, since she is established forever, but to assist, defend, and console her.

Viewed from another angle, Christ's Church also proceeds from the intercession of the Immaculate Heart of Mary Co-Redemptrix. At the very origin of her life, inseparable from the Passion of Christ, is the Compassion of Our Lady: *Stabat juxta Crucem.* It is solely with regard to the Catholic Church, to the exclusion of all others, that Mary exercises her spiritual maternity and rule. (She fulfils this unique and reserved role both through her intercession and her miraculous interventions.) Just as the Christ born of the Virgin in the stable at Bethlehem is not Nestorius' Christ in two persons, nor Eutyches' Christ of only one nature, and still less the modernists' humanitarian and enlightened figure, but rather the Only-Begotten Son of the Father, the Second Person of the Trinity who subsists in two natures, so too the Church, spiritually begotten by the Virgin at Calvary and preserved by the intercession of her Immaculate Heart, is not some vague universal gathering of all religious formations, but the one and only Catholic Church founded upon Peter and the apostles. She is the Church *of the confessors* who bore faithful witness to her immutable doctrine unto death; the Church *of the martyrs* who gave their lives for *the Creed and the Blessed Sacrament*; the Church *of the consecrated virgins* who are reserved for the Lord who is their Spouse. This alone is the Church of which Our Lady is Mother and Queen, Co-Redemptrix alongside the Redeemer: *Regina apostolorum et martyrum, confessorum et virginum.*

Having come from heaven, the Church returns thither in a continual and noble ascent each time one of the elect departs this land of exile. *Construitur in cælis vivis ex lapidibus.* Day by day, hour by hour, many of her children pass into glory. She sends them forth as envoys to the banquet of ineffable joy and unending thanksgiving. The moment they are united to God in the beatific vision, they become our mighty intercessors, their prayer unceasing and unwearied, until we too are admitted to the eternal wedding feast amidst the choirs of angels.

> *Nova veniens e cælo*
> *Nuptiali thalamo*
> *Præparata ut sponsata*
> *Copuletur Domino.*

"Having descended from heaven to return thither to celebrate the mystic nuptials, prepared as a bride, may she soon be united to her Lord!" She shall not be joined to Him without sharing in His Cross, praying and keeping vigil through His agony, which continues within her throughout the course of history. But through the Cross and through love, the Bridegroom knows how to unite His Bride to Himself with such gentleness and strength that nothing can ever separate them again. In the heavenly Jerusalem, it is by a *permanent* and unchanging disposition of love that God's elect take their blessed place, to the honour and glory of the Most Holy Trinity.

> *Disponuntur permansuri*
> *Sacris ædificiis.*

A Definitive Church

THE LORD FOUNDED HIS CHURCH not as a provisional religious institution, destined for endless and unfinished transformations, but as the definitive society of salvation, established once for all. She is endowed with the power to celebrate the worship of the New Law and to bring grace and truth to men, and, above all, with a charity which flows from the Cross and the seven sacraments, and which shall burn within her heart until the Parousia and through all eternity. Moreover, the mankind which the Church is charged to convert and to save is not the plaything of some shapeless and endless becoming. It indeed undergoes development, but it grows truly only insofar as it conforms itself to certain laws and remains within certain bounds. Should it scorn these laws—this natural law, let us say—and attempt, as the modern world does, to break through those bounds, the result is chaos, desolation, and a terrifying regression.

Thus we begin to perceive that it is not merely the perfection of her divine origin that requires the Church to be immutable and definitive, but also the enduring stability of the essential attributes of the human race, which she is charged and empowered to enlighten and save.

Thus Christ's Church—the Catholic Church, the one true Church—can proclaim supernatural truth to men only by respecting the proper laws of the human mind in the definition and transmission of that truth. Likewise, she can communicate grace through sacred signs only by adhering to the laws of signification that exist in human societies, and must therefore take care not to abandon these signs to purely individual whims. Nor could the Church rightly be called a society were she governed by a constitution that disregarded the demands of loyalty and justice proper to every normal human society. That is, her constitution, though entirely supernatural in origin, finds its analogy not in revolutionary régimes based on deceit and subversion, but in the honest governance of well-constituted earthly societies.

Obviously, the Church grows and develops. She makes her dogmas explicit, occasionally enriches the liturgy, and daily brings forth new saints. Yet she develops *in eodem sensu*:[1] in the same sense and along the same line. Thus the mustard seed becomes a vast tree capable of sheltering countless sparrows within its myriad branches when the furious storm breaks loose—but, in the end, the mighty tree remains a mustard tree.

There is no, and there shall be no, new Church. Absurd post-Conciliar fantasies or perverse modernist schemes shall alter nothing in this regard. Any Church that would claim to be new, setting itself against the Church of the first twenty Councils as the Church of *aggiornamento* does, is nothing but a pseudo-Church.

But let us now consider more closely at several key features of the Church's permanence, those more striking manifestations of her profound stability.

---

[1] St. Vincent of Lérins, *Commonitorium*, cited at length in Charles Cardinal Journet, *What is Dogma?*, trans. Mark Pontifex (San Francisco: Ignatius Press, 2011), especially in chapter 6, "The Life of Dogma."

As I have already said in previous studies,[2] fixity of *rite* is necessary to maintain validity of the *sacrament*. I speak of fixity of rite, not rigidity thereof, for in the order of grace, more even than in that of nature, laws, though immutable, are by no means inflexible:

> For interior and sacramental life
> Is not a thankless and constricted endeavour.[3]

But although fixity of rite allows for a certain latitude in formulas, language, and gestures, this latitude is limited and strictly conformed to the sacrament itself, according to the Redemptive Word of God. Such fixity is not rigidity, but a firm organization without harshness. With respect to gestures, language, and formulas, it was already in place during the earliest Christian centuries. Since then, it has been handed down faithfully, not with harshness or authoritarianism, but through a Tradition aided by the Holy Ghost and governed by the Magisterium. Those responsible for the anarchy of the new Mass saw fit to cast aside this venerable inheritance. They dismiss Latin, formulas, and postures. By means of hidden manipulation of dubious juridical weight,[4] they have altered the rites to such a degree that the congregation now appears to assume the role of principal celebrant, while the priest is reduced to a mere presider, scarcely distinguishable from the laity. As for the formulary, it has been so drastically revised that the Lutherans express delight.

The consequences of this liturgical upheaval have not been long in coming. The disastrous experiment, pursued with unwavering determination since the outset of the

---

[2] All my articles in the journal *Itinéraires* in 1970.
[3] Charles Péguy, "Ève."
[4] See, for instance, Abbé Raymond Dulac's "Témoignage," in *Itinéraires* 146 (September–October 1970), an issue dedicated to the holy sacrifice of the Mass.

present pontificate,[5] provides proof by way of negation that the validity of the *sacrament* instituted by God is inseparably bound to the stability of the *rite* put together by the Church. What, then, is to be done? Because the current pontificate, by its unprecedented innovations, compromises the Mass, the priest who believes in the Mass must, in this most essential matter, challenge the innovations of the current pontificate.

Let us now turn from the sacraments to the dogmas of the faith. Their formulas, wholly consonant with Sacred Scripture and Tradition, were gradually clarified and rigorously delimited to ward off the ambiguities and distortions of the heresiarchs. Thus: the Son is CONSUBSTANTIAL with the Father, not similar, as among men a son is only similar to his father and not one in being with him. MARY is MOTHER OF GOD, not merely the mother of Christ, as though Christ were not true God, the second Person of the Trinity made flesh for our salvation. In Christ, there is a DUALITY OF NATURES IN THE UNITY OF THE PERSON, not two persons mystically united, nor a personal unity brought about by the confusion or mingling of natures, but a harmonious union effected by the assumption of humanity by the Son of God. In this union, human nature is *filled with grace and truth* and elevated to the dignity of an *instrument conjoint* with the divinity. JUSTIFICATION OF THE SOUL is wrought not by an extrinsic imputation, but by a supernatural vivification penetrating to the very depths of man's freedom through a *grace at once healing and elevating.* THE SACRAMENTS ARE SACRED SIGNS THAT CONFER GRACE *EX OPERE OPERATO*, not merely pious gestures that stir fervour. ORIGINAL SIN is defined as a true fault, committed at

---

[5] Editor's note (1987): These lines were written in 1971.

the dawn of our history *by the first man and transmitted by generation to all his descendants*, save the Blessed Virgin. The presence of Christ in the Eucharist is a real presence brought about by TRANSUBSTANTIATION. The Mass is a TRUE SACRIFICE and the very same as that of Calvary by reason of the identity of both victim and priest, differing only in the mode of oblation.

These precise formulations of the faith, whereof I have cited but a few examples, are rendered all the more exact by the addition of anathemas. Such rigour is demanded by the nature of the human mind itself. For if the expression of revealed mysteries were left vague, indeterminate, and open to manifold interpretations, how could one prevent deviation, that is, heresy? And on the other hand, since the faith engages both our life and our eternal salvation, how could one commit his life, both in this temporal existence and for all eternity, to vagueness or approximation?

Clear and exact, and made yet more exact by the canons and anathemas that accompany them, the definitions of the faith are *irreformable*. What they present to our mind and propose for our assent is nothing other than the definitive Revelation brought to mankind by our Saviour: *omnia quæcumque audivi a Patre meo, nota feci vobis.*[6] Were these definitions subject to revision, it would mean either that the Revelation which they express is itself open to reform and thus not definitive, or that the elucidation provided by these definitions is not truly homogeneous with the revealed deposit. Both hypotheses are false.

To say that the definitions of the faith have been made more explicit over the course of the Church's history, which is true, is not to say that they are reformable, which

---

[6] "All things whatsoever I have heard of my Father, I have made known to you" (Jn 15:15).

is false. They have become explicit by developing their
meaning in *eodem sensu, in eadem sententia*, not by sub-
stituting one meaning for another. When one sees a rose
unfold at the first breezes of April or May, one does not
say that the rose reforms itself. If a grape in flower, so
fragile and tender in the gentle spring morrows, becomes a
heavy cluster by summer's end, it is not because the vine is
reformable, but because it is alive. So it is with the way the
dogmas become explicit over the ages: the dogma of the
Trinity and of the Incarnation; the doctrine concerning the
fall of man, the Blessed Sacrament, or the Blessed Virgin
Mary. Tradition transmits in a living manner. Sometimes
it makes things explicit, but it never transforms. Tradition
transmits, as living truth, those mysteries that are clearest
and most definitive. Hence the sharp precision of the formulas expressing revealed truth and of the anathemas that
bar the door to heretical interpretations. Tradition transmits the unchangeable and full divine truth—the divine,
supernatural, and total Revelation[7]—to human reason,
which remains itself unchangeable, as does our nature.
This is not to say that it remains motionless or incapable
of progress, but that it is unchangeable in its first intuitions
and grasp of fundamental principles.

This is precisely why the terms and concepts Tradition
adopts, elevates, and renders flexible for the supernatural mysteries are those immediately grasped by our mind,
common-sense terms and concepts[8] that any man naturally

---

[7] I have addressed this aspect of Revelation at length in *Théologie
de l'Histoire.*

[8] Are the theologians who break our heads with questions about
cultural eras and *reinterpretations* of language really unable to see
that *cultural age* does not change the truth? For a sound mind,
Christ's divinity will always mean, in every culture and every age,
the union, *within the one and only* divine Person, of human nature
with divine nature. The *real presence of Christ in the Eucharist* will

possesses unless he loses his reason, or unless, like our wayward modernists, he goes beyond truth and falsehood and thus extinguishes the primal lights that shine within a just heart. Indeed, the ideas and words serving as instruments for the definitions of the faith are drawn from common sense, albeit sometimes refined through philosophical elaboration. They are therefore accessible even to the humblest and least educated, for it suffices to be human, to have inherited human nature. It suffices to grasp, for example, what a person is, even if one cannot provide a reasoned exposition; to grasp also that beings possess a nature; that accidents differ from substance; that we possess freedom, and a freedom liable to fail; to grasp, in a word, the various notions employed by *the analogy of faith.*[9]

---

always mean, wherever and whenever, presence by a change of substance, with the accidents unchanged. *The perpetual virginity of Mary* will never mean anything other than the consecration of her virginity *ante partum, in partum,* and *post partum* by the Incarnate Word made her Son. The *way these mysteries are taught* may vary depending on the so-called *cultural age* of a people, but it is the same mysteries, according to the unchanging terms that define them, that are presented to minds that are, in essence, formed the same way. Cultural age changes nothing. The *Dutch Catechism,* which under the guise of adapting to our modern cultural age has altered both the content of these mysteries and the meaning of their defined terms, is a catechism of apostasy, and not ordinary apostasy, but modernist apostasy. Nothing more.

[9] It should be noted that the terms used in formulating the dogmas are often analogical: being, person, substance, nature, cause, grace, knowledge, love. These terms apply to God, angels, and men alike, but in very different ways. Thus, God is truly free, yet His freedom is infinitely higher than that of any creature, human or angelic. Similarly, it belongs to the infinite Being to be personal, but in the Holy Trinity, the terms "person" and "nature" are realized in a manner infinitely superior to what is found in any spiritual creature, *secundum quid idem, simpliciter diversum* (identical in a certain respect, but different, simply and purely speaking). This analogical scope of the terms expressing our faith is sometimes known by natural reason alone, as when we speak of God's wisdom or goodness, but more often it has been revealed to us by Revelation. For example,

It is both by a requirement of the natural human order
and by a demand of God's Revelation that the Church's
definitions are rigorous and irreformable. Yet the Second
Vatican Council, by its systematic refusal to define and
to anathematize,[10] has led many Christians into temptation, causing them to wonder whether true faith now lies
beyond the irreformable dogmas, or whether *pluralism*
in doctrine might henceforth be considered legitimate.
Twenty centuries of unchanging and living Tradition
compel us to answer with a categorical no. Even if the
twenty-first council were to contradict the twenty previous
ones, we will not waver. We will continue to study and
meditate on the definitions and anathemas already formulated. We will not cease to nourish our prayer by them, for
they alone bring us the Revelation of transcendent love:
Sic Deus dilexit mundum: God so loved the world that
He gave His only Son.[11]

---

if the Word of God had not made known to us all that He shares
with the Father, would we have dared to affirm that the one God is
Father, Son, and Holy Ghost? Or that the Son became incarnate in
Jesus? In any case, when the terms employed in the definitions of
the faith have an analogical meaning, the faithful experience no special difficulty in understanding them as true. They naturally grasp
that, if God is truly Father and Son, it is in the manner of God and
not that of men, and likewise with grace, charity, redemption, and
the Kingdom of God, which is Holy Church. Illuminating remarks
on analogy can be found at the end of the chapter "Metaphysical
Knowledge" in Jacques Maritain's *The Degrees of Knowledge*, trans.
Gerald B. Phelan et al. (New York: Charles Scribner's Sons, 1959).
See also some notes in our articles "La Joie des Saints" (*Itinéraires*, May 1969) and "La Sainte Église" (*Itinéraires*, November 1966,
especially pp. 145ff.)
[10] "Has the Second Vatican Council not itself welcomed the
demands made, among others, by Martin Luther, and through which
many aspects of the Christian life and faith are better expressed
now than before?" (Johannes Cardinal Willebrands, official delegate
of Paul VI to the Lutheran Congress of Evian, 14–24 July 1970).
[11] John 3:16. Hence, to proclaim, defend, and transmit the revealed
message in its purity and transcendence, dogmatic definitions and

Christian morality's honour lies in shutting down all excuses and closing every loophole. Why keep lying when the root of falsehood is cut off, rendered powerless, and put to death by the gift of grace that purifies and elevates? The new Law, which is the *law of grace,* has the glory of leading us to embrace divine morals by first mercilessly sorting out the impure and tangled desires of our fallen nature, and then attending solely to noble and good demands, drawing them into the pull of the theological virtues.

We admire in the saints the magnificent effects of grace, which have purified their hearts and transformed their innermost being. In contrast, we feel repelled and offended by the inner coarseness of heresiarchs, and if not always by their carnal weaknesses, at least by their unbridled pride *in spiritualibus.* It is enough, for example, to have read an accurate, even if brief, biography of Martin Luther to feel disgust at the spectacle of the sensual disarray of this married priest. Worse still, he was dominated by a pride so twisted that not only did he exempt himself from seeking forgiveness for his sins, but he also whitewashed and justified them by means of an aberrant interpretation of the Gospel. Luther's life and pretensions are too manifestly troubled and impure for us to ever admit that he "honestly and selflessly sought the message of the Gospel ... and that the demands he expressed reflect many aspects of Christian life and faith."[12]

What does it matter that it was the official envoy of the reigning pope who shared with us these incredible

---

anathemas are absolutely necessary. Let us add the practical necessity, at least within the Latin Rite Church, of *studying and using the Latin language* to ensure the orthodoxy of the faith and the validity of the sacraments. We intend to address this matter more fully in a separate study.

[12] In Cardinal Willebrands' text, cited above.

explanations about Luther's interior life! The dignity of
the messenger does not have the power to change reality,
and we believe none of the absurdities he seeks to impose
upon us. We are well versed enough in the immutable
precepts of natural law and the law of grace, revealed once
and for all, to be absolutely certain that Holy Church will
never yield to the troubled demands of the foul founder of
so-called Reformed religion. The Church will never open
the way to a spiritual life that tries to reconcile Christ
with Belial.[13]

Thus, two inseparable and indelible marks always shine
forth in every aspect of the Church, whether her governance, holiness, doctrine, or liturgy. First, the intrinsically
supernatural character of this hierarchical society of grace,
and second, its consonance and perfect harmony with the
just laws of our immutable nature.

---

[13] 2 Cor 6:15.

3

Dogmatic Definitions
and Ritual Order

T HE DEFINITIONS OF THE FIRST
twenty councils, which are protected by anathemas, clarified but did not alter the deposit of Revelation. These clarifications—concerning the mysteries of
the one God in three Persons, the Incarnation, the Virgin
Mary, original sin, and, in short, the development of our
entire faith—are rigorously consistent with the Word of
God. Nicaea, Ephesus, Chalcedon, Orange[1] express the
same truths as the four Gospels, the Acts of the Apostles,
the Epistles, and the Apocalypse. They do so in response
to new errors, employing new terms which, without harm-
ing the language of Scripture in the slightest, serve to cir-
cumscribe its content with utmost clarity and honesty.

The first twenty councils cannot mislead because they
adopted the surest means of not misleading: defining the
truth. Not content with merely defining and driven, as
it were, by an abundance of candor, these councils took
pains to articulate the opposing proposition explicitly, the

---

[1] The provincial synod held in 529 under Saint Caesarius, whose
decisions were taken up by the Ecumenical Council of Trent.

better to reject it with a carefully formulated anathema.
Consider, for example, the famous decrees of Trent on
the Eucharist, the Mass, and the priesthood. It would be
hard to exercise greater care in preventing any equivocation or ambiguity. Such is the essence of honest language.
Est, est; non, non.

> If anyone says that after the consecration is com-
> pleted, the body and blood of Our Lord Jesus
> Christ are not in the admirable sacrament of
> the Eucharist, but are there only *in usu*, while
> being taken and not before or after, and that
> in the hosts or consecrated particles which are
> reserved or which remain after communion, the
> true body of the Lord does not remain, let him
> be anathema.[2]

> If anyone says that in the holy sacrament of the
> Eucharist, Christ, the only begotten Son of God,
> is not to be adored with the worship of *latria*,
> also outwardly manifested, and is consequently
> neither to be venerated with a special festive
> solemnity, nor to be solemnly borne about in
> procession according to the laudable and uni-
> versal rite and custom of holy Church, or is
> not to be set publicly before the people to be
> adored and that the adorers thereof are idolaters,
> let him be anathema.[3]

> If anyone says that in the Mass a true and real
> sacrifice is not offered to God; or that to be
> offered is nothing else than that Christ is given
> to us to eat, let him be anathema.[4]

---

[2] Trent, Canon 4 on the Most Holy Sacrament of the Eucharist (in
Canons and Decrees of the Council of Trent, trans. H. J. Schroeder
[St. Louis: B. Herder, 1960], 79).
[3] Trent, Canon 6 on the Most Holy Sacrament of the Eucharist
(in *Canons and Decrees*, 80).
[4] Trent, Canon 1 on the Sacrifice of the Mass (in *Canons and
Decrees*, 149).

> If anyone says that by those words, "Do this for a commemoration of me" (Luke 22:19; 1 Corinthians 11:24), Christ did not institute the apostles priests; or did not ordain that they and other priests should offer His own body and blood, let him be anathema.[5]

> If anyone says that the sacrifice of the Mass is one only of praise and thanksgiving; or that it is a mere commemoration of the sacrifice consummated on the Cross but not a propitiatory one; or that it profits him only who receives, and ought not to be offered for the living and the dead, for sins, punishments, satisfactions, and other necessities, let him be anathema.[6]

> If anyone says that order or sacred ordination is not truly and properly a sacrament instituted by Christ the Lord, or that it is some human contrivance devised by men unskilled in ecclesiastical matters, or that it is only a certain rite for choosing ministers of the word of God and of the sacraments, let him be anathema.[7]

After that, a mere glance at the documents of Vatican II reveals that the Fathers have decidedly broken with the Tradition of clear and unequivocal language. I am not unaware of the few vigorously formal texts, such as the *nota prævia* that corrects certain vague and dangerous developments in *Lumen Gentium* regarding the power of bishops. Nevertheless, it remains true, first, that even the admirable *nota prævia* does not present itself as a definition of faith and carries no anathema; and secondly, and more critically, that the usual style of expression proper to

---

[5] Trent, Canon 2 on the Sacrifice of the Mass (*ibid.*).
[6] Trent, Canon 2 on the Sacrifice of the Mass (*ibid.*).
[7] Trent, Canon 3 on the Sacrament of Order (in *Canons and Decrees*, 163).

Vatican II is imprecise, verbose, and even evasive. What, for example, is the political and social teaching of the Catholic Church according to the twenty-first council? Whereas the *Syllabus* and the encyclicals from Leo XIII to Pius XII set it forth clearly, *Gaudium et Spes* and *Dignitatis Humanæ* leave us mired in vagueness and uncertainty.

But why should we be surprised? It is well established that these texts are the products of compromise. It is equally established that a modernist faction sought to impose heretical doctrines. Though prevented from fully succeeding, it nonetheless managed to have non-formal texts adopted. These texts offer modernism a double advantage: they cannot be accused of expressing blatantly heretical propositions, but remain open to interpretations that contradict the faith.

Should we hold off challenging them? We once considered it. The difficulty is that they offer no grounds for argumentation; they are too slippery. When one tries to press a formula that seems troubling, one finds on the very same page another formula that is entirely irreproachable. When one tries to support one's preaching or teaching with a solid text, one that cannot be twisted and effectively conveys to one's audience the traditional content of faith and morals, it soon becomes evident that the chosen passage —on the liturgy or on society's duty toward the true religion, for instance—is insidiously weakened by a second text which, though appearing to complement the first, in reality undermines it. Decrees follow constitutions, and messages follow declarations, without giving the mind, save for very rare exceptions, sufficient foothold.

Objection: for pastoral reasons and to bring back those who have strayed, a method that defines and condemns is unsuitable. Fair enough. But is there an honest alternative? Without clear definitions, one shall only lead wandering souls into vagueness and ambiguity. I struggle to see how one can claim to practice true pastoral care in this way, seeking the good of souls, truth for the mind, and conversion for the heart.

Certainly, whenever I encounter a "separated brother," I will explain the content of the faith as well as I can, tailoring my approach to address his difficulties. However, my explanations must be anchored in and guided by the definitions. While I need not employ the impersonal, abstract style of formal definitions to convey the revealed deposit, I will endeavour to meet my interlocutor where he stands. Yet I will also ensure that my adaptations do not backfire on the definitions themselves, dulling their sharpness even slightly. Under the pretext of pastoral adaptation, softening a dogmatic formula one seeks to explain is to divert souls from the very truth whither one intends to guide them.

Suppose you are having a conversation with a Protestant seeking clarity on the mystery of the priesthood. You would begin by stating the Catholic position, recalling the decrees of the Council of Trent. Then you would surely proceed to examine the Scriptural texts concerning the priesthood. You might continue by agreeing with your interlocutor on the existence of a common priesthood shared by all the baptized: men, women, and even those poor souls deprived of reason but reborn in Christ. You would probably also acknowledge regrettable abuses in some celebrations of the Mass that casually neglect the assembly and seem to disregard the common priesthood of the faithful. Nevertheless, you would plead mitigating circumstances, observing that no rite, however wisely instituted and attentive to all, has endured for two millennia without some lapses or negligence. Yet, after all manner of research, confrontation, explanation, and exegesis, you

will be forced, unless you deceive your Protestant interlocutor, to return to the starting point, the definition you
were debating, which cannot be moved or softened:

> If anyone says that there is not in the New Tes
> tament a visible and external priesthood, or that
> there is no power of consecrating and offering the
> true Body and Blood of the Lord and of forgiving
> and retaining sins, but only the office and bare
> ministry of preaching the Gospel; or that those
> who do not preach are not priests at all, let him
> be anathema.[8]

> If anyone says that order or sacred ordination is
> not truly and properly a sacrament instituted by
> Christ the Lord, or that it is some human con
> trivance devised by men unskilled in ecclesias
> tical matters, or that it is only a certain rite for
> choosing ministers of the word of God and of the
> sacraments, let him be anathema.[9]

> If anyone says that by sacred ordination the Holy
> Ghost is not imparted and that therefore the bish
> ops say in vain: "Receive ye the Holy Ghost," or
> that by it a character is not imprinted, or that he
> who has once been a priest can again become a
> layman, let him be anathema.[10]

Only the priesthood of an ordained priest possesses a
power that, though astonishing, is no less real and precisely
defined: to offer the Holy Sacrifice through the separate
transubstantiation of bread and wine. The priesthood of
the merely baptized does not come close to this power in
any way. It is distinct and operates in an entirely different

---

[8] Trent, Canon 1 on the Sacrament of Order (in *Canons and Decrees*, 162–163).
[9] Trent, Canon 3 on the Sacrament of Order (in *Canons and Decrees*, 163).
[10] Trent, Canon 4 on the Sacrament of Order (*ibid.*).

sphere. This stems ultimately from the fact that the Church, being hierarchically constituted by divine institution, grants certain powers to some of her members, but not indiscriminately to all. Furthermore, by virtue of this same divine institution, these powers are conferred personally and not delegated to a collective body, nor determined by the majority vote or democratic consultation of the people of God.

Let us have kindness, patience, understanding, and agility of mind in listening and explaining, but at the same time, and above all, unyielding rigour in presenting the definitions of the faith. These have always been, from the beginning, the double principles of Catholic pastoral care. We have no desire to alter this, even if the most recent Council claimed to offer a better approach. Our pastoral efforts shall therefore continue to rely firmly on the preceding councils which deliberately chose to define and distinguish truth from error, thereby adopting the only means of leading the flock to wholesome pastures and accomplishing pastoral work worthy of its name.

We certainly desire the return of Protestants to Catholic integrity and unity. But let this return be achieved with honour, free from equivocations. Protestants must be warned from the outset, among other things, that the Church regards their communion as a corruption of the evangelical institution and consequently demands that they renounce it. Similarly, in the same spirit and need for honesty, we will tell Muslims that the Church of Jesus Christ acknowledges as the one true God not theirs, but His and ours; not the God who excludes from His mystery the Trinity of Persons and the Incarnation of the Son, not the God of Caiaphas and the enigmatic founder of Islam,[11]

---

[11] See Father Gabriel Théry (Hanna Zacharias), O. P., *L'Islam, Entreprise Juive*, especially volume 4 (Cahors: self-published, 1955).

but the God of Abraham and Jesus Christ. For Abraham, though he did not yet know the Trinity of Persons, worshipped their unity with such submission and love that he was prepared to receive the full Revelation concerning Yahweh; that is, to believe explicitly in the Holy Trinity. Let us remember, indeed, the profound words of Jesus, the Incarnate Word: "Your father Abraham rejoiced to see my day; he saw it and was glad" (John 8:56).

The Gospel always inclines toward greater clarity. It is infinitely mysterious, but nonetheless demands that we form a precise understanding of its mystery. Each verse is an invitation to open ourselves to the divine light and to become as keenly aware as possible of the ineffable Revelation: *Sic Deus dilexit mundum*: God so loved the world that He gave His only Son.[12]

To be heard as it truly is, the Gospel cannot do without formal conciliar definitions, and these definitions in turn are rooted in the Gospel, blossoming from the very letter of Scripture. These definitions are not always the fruit of exegetical glosses, but it remains true that it is assiduous meditation on the entirety of the Scriptures by the contemplative and theological Church that gave rise to dogmatic definitions. And because they are destined for the salvation of all, the Church formulated them in the two languages best suited to convey universal truths, the languages *par excellence* of the *logos*: Greek and Latin.

Most Sunday homilies nowadays are disappointingly shallow, reeking of vague sentimentality, merely paraphrasing the Gospel or veering into simplistic, revolutionary political tangents. This is largely because preachers have forgotten both dogmatic definitions and the plain answers of the catechism when pondering the sacred texts. Their

---

[12] John 3:16.

reflections have not been guided by faith at all, or only weakly so, because they have neglected the proper means, namely, recourse to the definitions of the faith. The remedy to this lamentable poverty in so-called "Biblical" sermons is not to abandon the Gospel commentary in favour of the catechism or doctrinal formulas alone, but rather to keep the catechism's answers and the major conciliar explanations in mind when engaging in a reflective reading of the Gospel.

In the Catholic Church, we have three essential books, albeit not on the same level: the Bible, the Missal,[13] and the Catechism; that is, the Bible together with the Missal and the Catechism. To them each one may add, according to his capacity, some spiritual authors, perhaps some excerpts from the Church Fathers, the *Enchiridion Symbolorum et Definitionum*, or the *Summa Theologica*.[14]

The study of the Bible, particularly of the New Testament, constantly invites us to turn to the dogmatic definitions, or more simply, to the answers of the catechism, in order to grasp the text in its full depth. Let us take, for example, Saint Luke's account of the Annunciation. We see the Archangel Gabriel enter, and we hear him greet Mary, "full of grace." We are struck by that great question: "How shall this be, since I know not man?" We are still more filled with wonder at the answer: "The Holy Ghost shall come upon thee, and the power of the Most High shall overshadow thee, and therefore the Child that shall be born of thee shall be holy, and shall be called the Son of God"!

---

[13] The Missal up to Pius XII inclusive, and indeed, at a pinch, up to the death of John XXIII.

[14] A certain number of articles in Saint Thomas' *Summa*, and sometimes an entire question, whether from the *Prima Pars*, the *Secunda* or especially the *Tertia*, are within the reach of Christians who have received a solid doctrinal formation.

Now, once we have finished reading the chapter and are entirely steeped in the charm of its heavenly beauty, we are unlikely to plunge at once into Denzinger's collection to look up the anathemas of the Council of Ephesus. Each thing in its proper time. First, let us linger in the simplicity of God's Word as the Gospel presents it, allowing its truth to penetrate our hearts without haste or commentary. In due course, we may turn to the councils—I mean the councils prior to Vatican II—to study, according to our ability, the explanations and clarifications furnished by the divinely assisted solemn Magisterium. In this way, we shall enter more deeply and with full confidence into the text of Scripture.

We shall find, in particular, that if we conclude that the formulas of Ephesus concerning Mary as Theotokos missed the mark, then it would follow that Saint Luke's account missed the reality, being no more than a harmonious but empty tale, a seductive but unreal message. In truth, however, it is the historical and factual account of the Word of God's Incarnation, the message of salvation through Jesus Christ, who became man thanks to the *fiat* of Mary ever-virgin.

The tiresome dichotomy that sets defined dogma against the pure Gospel is illusory. One calls for the other. Hence, there must be a frequent back-and-forth between the letter of Scripture and the formulas of the councils and the Catechism. Let us move from the letter of the Old or New Testament to the conciliar or pontifical definitions in order to grasp more fully the exact meaning and true scope of the sacred text. Then, let us return from the councils and the Catechism to the simple text of Scripture, so as never to lose sight of the living, concrete, and supernaturally inexhaustible reality, whose depth and mystery the formulations of the ecclesiastical Magisterium express with all due precision.

Because we believe that the content of the Gospel is as precise as possible, and because we desire to proclaim it in all its truth, as pastors worthy of the name ought to do, we intend never to separate the Gospel texts from the defined propositions, the books of Scripture from the lessons of the catechism, or meditations on the Gospel from reflections on the anathemas.

The Church preserves the deposit both of the sacramental *sign* instituted by Christ and of the *ritual* order that manifests the sign and surrounds it with honour. As guardian of the sacramental sign, she keeps it intact and immutable, for it belongs properly to the Lord Jesus. He Himself who established it once and for all during His earthly life; and it is He again who, every day in heavenly glory, confers upon it its efficacy.

The Church is also the guardian of the ritual order, fixing it with the assistance of the Holy Ghost and defending it once set. Any changes she introduces—adapted to specific times, regions, dioceses, or religious orders—are carefully measured to maintain the validity of the sacramental rite and to celebrate it with utmost devotion. Such changes, therefore, remain within strict limits.

In many cases, it appears that these changes aim to reverse the drift into routine, to cleanse the ceremonies of an almost inevitable accumulation of grime, and to put an end to the consequences of either lukewarmness or individual arbitrariness that had come to assume the force of rubrics. *Changes* of this nature, far from weakening tradition, give free rein to its profound life, restoring the purity of its source while maintaining intact its rightful gains accumulated over the centuries.

For these changes to be effective, they must be enacted with moderation and supported by the fervour of both clergy and faithful. At Mass, the Nicene Creed ought not to vary according to time or place, for it defines the Catholic faith, which is identical for all and at all times. Nor ought the consecratory formula to vary, since it constitutes the sacramental sacrifice, which Our Lord instituted once and for all. The Canon, intimately tied to the immutable consecration and guarded by venerable tradition, cannot be altered without grave impiety. Similarly, the offertory, though not a dogmatic definition or sacramental sign, is so closely linked to the consecration's sacrificial meaning that it demands preservation. As for the other parts of the Mass, assuming some changes might be desirable, they must be exceptional, and the Pope would be justified in permitting them only for very grave, just, and holy reasons. Needless to say, changes must never aim to curry favour with Protestants or, as Paul VI ventured, create a polyvalent Mass adaptable to their rites.

Diviserunt sibi vestimenta mea (John 19:24). Today, it is the priests of Jesus Christ, not the soldiers of Pilate, who divide the garments of the crucified King. By destroying the unity and stability of the rites handed down by Tradition and manipulating them according to their whims and fancies, these priests of the Lord endanger the sacramental institution that is indivisible and universal. Indeed, through their sacrilegious alterations they may have already destroyed its effects, insofar as lies within their power. Yet Jesus' tunic, which was woven seamlessly from top to bottom, was not divided. Though cast by lot, it remained undivided and whole. This tunic, which some pious authors report was woven by the very hands of Our Lady, is the faithful image of the sumptuous robe of the sacred rites that the Church's Tradition has, from the very beginning, woven all around the sacramental signs, especially all around Jesus' Eucharistic Body.

The Church has fashioned and arranged these garments of glory not without the special intercession of the Virgin

Mary, our Mother and Mediatrix. And the same intercession of the Immaculate Virgin will obtain for the Church
the preservation of their integrity and nobility. Though
evil prelates may threaten and persecute those who maintain the rite in order to preserve the sacrament, they cannot prevent the Catholic Church from raising up, even to
the end of time, laymen, priests, bishops, and popes who
will preserve, by virtue of their faith in the sacraments,
the unity and stability of the ritual order. Thus will they
keep whole and undivided the seamless robe.

4

Authority and Holiness in the Church

O NE WOULD HAVE TO DO VIO- lence to the Gospel, the Acts of the Apostles, the Epistles, and even the Apocalypse to conclude from them that authority and hierarchy are not essential to the Church founded by Our Lord. The word "hierarchy" may lack a particularly mystical resonance; it may irritate not only our pride but also our sense of honesty, given how often we have been saturated with abuses of power or the incapacity of leaders. At first glance, the term may even seem incompatible with *holiness* itself. Yet the Gospel— which is essentially *mystical*, for it reveals to us, among other wonders, what human life is when wholly immersed in the *mysteries of God* in Christ Jesus—is at once the full Revelation of holiness and indivisibly the full Rev- elation of a certain authority. This authority is endowed with powers befitting holiness: the power to administer the sacraments (especially the Most Holy Sacrament); the power to proclaim infallibly those truths which are God's own secrets, namely the supernatural mysteries; and finally, the power to ordain priests who, by virtue of the sacrament of order and under a defined jurisdiction, will themselves be capable in turn of preaching the mysteries and administering the sacraments.

Consider what happens when one attempts to remove from the Gospel the choosing of the Twelve, the primacy of Peter among the Twelve, the ordination of the apostles alone to consecrate the bread and wine into the Body and Blood of the Son of God offered for us; in short, the institution of a rigorously constituted hierarchy. One thus removes the Gospel itself. One subjects it to an amputation so vast that it becomes unrecognizable and unable to sustain itself. The Protestants attempted precisely this. But the falsehood of the thesis which seeks to retain the Gospel's mysticism and holiness while removing authority and hierarchy has been demonstrated twenty times over.

If we read the Gospel as it is actually written, seeking first to see what truly is, however much discomfort or torment this may cause us,[1] we are compelled to acknowledge that Gospel affirms the reality of the Church, and conversely, the Church, whose existence and constitution the Gospel guarantees to us, is a hierarchical society of supernatural life, or, to put it another way, a society both supernatural and hierarchical of life with God.

Fair enough. But ever since Jesus himself rebuked Peter, we have all known that in the Church—*Holy* Church— those who hold authority are not always saints. Far from it. And perhaps we have experienced all too abundantly the crushing truth of Jesus' condemnation of the chief of the Apostles: *Vade post me, Satana.* Too often, those in authority—priests, bishops, the pope, each at their respective

---

[1] "Two kinds of persons know [religion]: those who have a humble heart, and who love lowliness, whatever kind of intellect they may have, high or low; and those who have sufficient understanding to see the truth, whatever opposition they may have to it" (Blaise Pascal, *Pensées*, 288 in Brunschvicg's numbering, trans. W. F. Trotter [New York: The Modern Library, 1941], 98).

level—commit sins that are manifestly grave, even horrible sins of tyranny, pride, jealousy, cowardice, and lust, all
while disguising them under respectable or even sublime
masks. Worse still, as we witness today, some go so far as
to subvert the very form of authority established by Our
Lord Himself. In His Church, Our Lord wanted personal
authority and instituted it as personal. Yet since the Council we have witnessed a gigantic attempt to strip away this
authority. What is personal by divine right, we now see
being parliamentarized, collegialized, and one might even
say sovietized.

Let me explain what I mean. One can turn over every
single page of the Gospel, and nowhere will one find that
the teaching of the faith is entrusted to some commission
that operates independently of the hierarchy, with bishops
and priests serving merely as delegates and executors. I am
not exaggerating. And if this is not how things work in the
new Church that Vatican II attempted to establish, then
explain this to me: Why does some "good" bishop who
teaches his great-nephews a proper Catholic catechism—
complete with Mary ever-virgin, the Holy Sacrifice of
the Mass, original sin, and the holy angels—nevertheless
impose upon the tens of thousands of children in his diocese a catechism produced by committees, in which all
these dogmas are either denied or so muddled as to be
unrecognizable? Why? Because this "good" bishop has
been stripped of his episcopal authority by collegiality, and
he attempts, in private and as a great-uncle, to recover
himself and silence the unbearable pangs of his episcopal
conscience. The same observation applies to the "passable"
bishop who would certainly be horrified at the thought
that his young cousin, whose marriage he officiated, might
not hesitate to use the pill, yet who finds nothing horrible
about authorizing, as head of his diocese and for tens of

thousands of young women and wives, these diabolical contraceptives.

Our Lord Jesus, true God and true man, has founded a holy Church, a society at the level of the mysteries and holiness of the one God in three persons: *et societas nostra sit cum Patre et cum Filio ejus, Jesu Christo.*[2] He has endowed this Church with particular powers directed toward holiness. These powers are hierarchical, divinely assisted, and personal. Hierarchical, because they involve degrees, mutual ordering, a right to command, and a duty to obey (in short, a *juris dictio*, a real capacity to *declare what is right*). Divinely assisted, because these powers are guaranteed by the action of the Holy Ghost against dogmatic heresy and sacramental invalidity. Personal, because these powers are held by a particular person (whether common or noble, holy, or mediocre), a person who is personally responsible. They cannot be transferred to any of those multiple types of Rousseauist and Masonic organization, in which real power is hidden and masked while the person who officially holds power is stripped of actual authority and transformed into a mere agent of execution.

The false Church that has manifested itself among us since the curious Second Vatican Council noticeably departs, year after year, from the Church founded by Jesus Christ. The false post-Conciliar Church stands increasingly in direct opposition to the holy Church that has saved souls for twenty centuries (and, moreover, has enlightened and sustained the city). The pseudo-Church now in the making is ever more directly opposed to the true Church, the only Church of Christ, through the strangest innovations both in hierarchical constitution and in doctrine and morals.

---

[2] "And our society is with the Father and with His Son, Jesus Christ" (1 John 1:3).

What is to be done? This priest, the son of Saint Dominic who writes these lines, knows full well that he cannot take the place of any of those priests of the first order who have entered into the *apostolic succession*. Indeed, he never had any desire or ambition to do so. I am a Dominican and ask for nothing more. May it please God and Our Lady to grant me fidelity to the end. That is all.

Therefore, we priests cannot take the place of bishops, any more than bishops can make themselves pope. What is absurd and criminal about collegiality is that this organization of a democratic,[3] Masonic, and Rousseauist sort essentially "papifies" the bishops. We have bishops who are personally nullified but who are, collegially, in the process of being "papified."

Whatever may be said of the aberrations of hierarchical authority in Holy Church and of the novelty of collegialist thinking behind these aberrations, priests of the second order cannot take the place of bishops, nor can laymen take the place of priests. Are we then to dream about establishing some immense, worldwide league or association of priests and faithful Christians who, having become "credible interlocutors" with the official hierarchy, might force it to take back the reins and restore order? A grandiose design, and moving, but a chimerical one. For ultimately, this group would claim to be of the Church but would be neither diocese nor archdiocese, neither parish nor religious order. It would fit into none of the sectors within which and for which authority is exercised in Holy Church. It would be an artificial group: an *arte factum* foreign to the real, established, and recognized groups. As with any collective, a problem of leadership and authority would arise therein, and all the more acutely as it grows.

---

[3] I speak, as can be understood from context, of historical and Rousseauist democracy.

We would soon have a group that, being an association, cannot evade the question of authority, but its being artificial (and therefore outside associations according to nature and according to Revelation and grace) would render the question of authority insoluble. Rival groups would not be slow to arise. War would become inevitable. There would exist between the rival groups no canonical means of ending this war or even of conducting it.

Are we then condemned to impotence amid often sacrilegious chaos? I do not believe so. First, by virtue of belonging to Jesus Christ, the Church is assured with absolute certainty that she will preserve, until the very end of the world, enough authentic personal hierarchy to maintain the seven sacraments, particularly the Sacraments of the altar and Holy Orders, and to ensure that the unique and invariable doctrine of salvation continues to be preached and taught. "Behold, I am with you all days, *even to the consummation of the world.*"[4] "For as often as you shall eat this bread, and drink the chalice, you shall show the death of the Lord, *until He come.*"[5] "And unless those days had been shortened, no flesh should be saved; but for the sake of the elect those days shall be shortened."[6] These texts say what they say, namely, the certainty of an invincible permanence of the Church in teaching, sacrament, and holiness, and they do not suffer desperate or despairing reinterpretations.

Furthermore, even amid the progressive diminishment—albeit always limited—of real personal hierarchical authority, we all possess, priests and laymen alike, each for our own account, a small share of authority. We priests have the powers to celebrate the true Mass, to absolve, and to preach.

---

[4] Matthew 28:20.
[5] 1 Corinthians 11:26.
[6] Matthew 24:22.

Parents, despite state totalitarianism and the breakdown
of society, have not lost all power to form and educate the
children they have brought into the world. One could make
similar observations about schools and those responsible for
them: priests, brothers, religious sisters, or laymen.

Therefore, let the faithful priest who is capable of
instructing, preaching, absolving, and saying Mass, exert
himself to the full extent of his power and grace to preach,
instruct, forgive sins, and offer the Holy Sacrifice in the
traditional rite.[7] Let the teaching sister exert herself to
the full extent of her grace and power to form young
women in faith, good morals, purity, and literature. Let
each priest, each layman, each small group of laymen and
priests, holding authority and power over a small fortress
of Church and Christendom, exert themselves to the full
extent of their possibilities and power. Let the leaders of
these fortresses and their occupants not ignore one another
but communicate among themselves. Let each of these fortresses, protected, defended, trained, and directed in its
prayer and chants by real authority, become as far as possible a bastion of holiness. This is what shall ensure the certain continuity of the true Church and effectively prepare
a restoration for the day that shall please the Lord. This
is how one prepares, and not through the vast machinery
of worldwide associations, for which the problem of leadership will remain insoluble while aspirations to holiness
vanish into frivolous chatter and are smothered under the
multiplicity of circulars and bulletins, not to mention the
lamentable proliferation of meetings and congresses.

Whatever may come of the diabolical experiments of the
new post-Vatican Church, it shall always remain possible
and assured in the Church to strive for holiness in reality

---

[7] It goes without saying that the exercise of these powers is not
invalidated by a *vacatio legis* when it occurs in the Church.

and to learn the immutable and supernatural doctrine in a real community, even a very small one, under real authority. The Church shall always ensure the presence of true priests and faithful bishops who have not abdicated their responsibilities, knowingly or unknowingly, into the hands of committees and collegiality.

This means, it seems to me, that the most effective way to allow the Christian struggle fully to flourish while escaping internal conflicts and external rivalries is to conduct it through small units that know one another insofar as they are able and come to each other's aid when occasion arises, but refuse to enter into systematic and universal organizations of any sort. In these various units—such as a modest school, a humble convent, a pious confraternity, a small grouping of Christian families, or a pilgrimage organization—authority is real and undisputed; the problem of leadership scarcely arises; the work to be done is clear. It is simply a matter of exercising one's grace and authority to the fullest within the small sphere whereof one certainly has charge, while remaining connected, without great administrative machinery, to those who are doing likewise.

Our Lord will shatter collegiality, grant us bishops who will exercise their powers personally and in holiness, and raise up a great and holy pope when He sees in His Church souls and groups fervent enough to welcome them. Until then, He will not permit collegiality and democratization ever to prevail. He will not permit it because He will always give to His Church, in order for her to remain holy—that is, to perform the sacraments and sanctify souls—the indispensable measure of hierarchical power and ordinary priestly power. Our Lady assumed into heaven, who never ceases to intercede for the Church of her Son, is always certain to be heard. It is fitting to say to her: *Regina pastorum omnium, ora pro nobis.*

5

The Church's Governance and Sanctification

I N THE NEW TESTAMENT, THE
Church is only a mustard seed, and does not yet
appear to us as a great tree. Her proper mystery
is nevertheless revealed to us with sufficient clarity as
to leave no doubt as to her hierarchical constitution and
the personal status of her powers. The power of supreme
rule and sovereign jurisdiction is conferred on the Vicar of
Christ alone and not on a synod, on Peter alone and not
on an assembly.[1] The power to offer the Holy Sacrifice is
not given to all indiscriminately, but to the apostles alone
and to those Christians whom they ordain. Jurisdiction
over the particular churches of which Saint Paul's Epistles often speak belongs to a specific bishop, and not to a
committee composed of laymen and clerics.

Unlike the case with earthly cities, the powers granted
to the Holy City in the Kingdom of God aim towards
a transcendent and celestial object, an order of divine
realities and a truly supernatural common good. "Going
therefore, teach ye all nations, baptizing them in the name

---

[1] See Appendix 3, "On the Church and the Pope."

of the Father, and of the Son, and of the Holy Ghost."[2]
"I will give to thee the keys of the Kingdom of Heaven."[3]
"This do ye for the commemoration of me. For as often as
you shall eat this bread, and drink the chalice, you shall
shew the death of the Lord, until He come."[4]

What is called into question nowadays is not only the
transcendent and supernatural scope of the powers granted
to the Church, but also, and perhaps more acutely, their
personal attribution. Now, divine ordinance, against which
we can do nothing, has willed that, in the Church, powers
be personally attributed. The democratic and Rousseauist
assembly system of government is foreign to the Kingdom
of God. Even councils are no exception. For while it is
true that, in these great ecumenical gatherings, it is the
bishops as a body who define (except at Vatican II) and
who legislate, their decisions carry authority only when
sanctioned by the Sovereign Pontiff, and the authority of
each bishop over his diocese is in no way suspended by
virtue of the council, nor transferred to the episcopal body.

Rousseauist-type democracy is a system of governance
conceived and applied in such a way that numbers take
precedence over right, allowing the true leaders, those
who in fact exercise authority, to be usually able to evade
responsibility. In effect, the official holders of power are
hypocritically dispossessed of effective power, and the reality of power is transferred to parallel authorities that are
irresponsible and elusive. In this sense, Rousseauist democracy is a régime of falsehood.[5] It is even more intolerable

---

[2] Matthew 28:19.

[3] Matthew 16:19.

[4] 1 Corinthians 11:25–26.

[5] On these questions, see the following particularly vigorous, if
incomplete, books: Charles Maurras, *La Démocratie Religieuse*;
Augustin Cochin, *Les Sociétés de Pensée et la Démocratie*; Cochin,
La Révolution et la Libre-Pensée. Maurras's thought is not, in its

in Holy Church—in the Kingdom of all truth—than in
the kingdoms of this world.

Moreover, one need only see the democratic system of
collegiality at work to be persuaded of its hypocrisy and
its intrinsic malice. After only a few years, what fruits has
the collegial system borne? A falsified catechism thanks
to the *Fonds Obligatoire*,[6] a perverted marriage morality
thanks to Note 16,[7] a Mass rendered equivocal, sometimes
invalid, often sacrilegious, thanks to unbridled ritual innovations. And in all this, there is nothing, absolutely nothing
for which one can safely lay direct blame upon any given
bishop, as one can upon Martin Luther for the initiative
of having married priests.

In the revolutionary upheavals now ravaging the Church
of France, which were inconceivable only ten years ago,
everything is imposed by a headless power, acting collegially, under the anonymity of crushing majorities. Whom
should we blame and how should we judge? In promulgating the *Fonds Obligatoire* or Note 16, the collegial assembly
of Lourdes was not carrying out an immediate and explicit
order from the Holy See. Shall we accuse this bishop, that
archbishop, that cardinal? But why this one rather than
that one? They are all submerged in the assembly. It is the
assembly that wanted this destruction of faith, morals and
worship. The assembly, that is, everyone and no one. The
assembly ratified, by an overwhelming vote, propositions

---

essence, Christian. Nevertheless, many of his political views, includ-
ing those touching on religion, are admirably sound and penetrating.
It is proper to make use of them in the light of the faith. See also
Appendix 2, "Sons of the Church in a Time of Trial."

[6] Translators' note: A catechism published by the French epis-
copate in 1967.

[7] The Note by which, in October 1968, the collegial assembly of
Lourdes candidly rejected the prescriptions and prohibitions of
Humanæ vitæ. See *Itinéraires* 128 (December 1968).

elaborated in the small groups of theologians by majority vote. From the assembly to the commissions, from the commissions to the small groups, from the small groups to the restricted committees, there was always at hand a convenient means of shifting responsibility, without ever being able to discover precisely who first set the ball rolling, or to what exact end. Only the goal, the demolition of religion, was certain. At each of the collegial plenary assemblies, the destruction of doctrine, morals and liturgy has made considerable progress. But who is the destroyer? All the bishops or nearly so, if one considers the mechanism of majority vote, but a small number difficult to identify, if one considers personal determination, maturely reflected upon and calculated. And herein lies the hypocrisy and unnaturalness of the collegial system: it relieves each bishop as far as possible of the weight of personal responsibility and the intolerable fire of remorse, yet by the same mechanism makes each one an accomplice in the gravest crimes, in erecting a pseudo-Christian religion under the mask of Christianity.

Well! The collegial system does nothing but extend to the Church the misdeeds of Rousseauist democracy. Were it to continue for a few more years, the Church would be drained of her divine powers to infallibly transmit Revelation, celebrate the true Mass, confer the true sacraments, and ensure valid ordinations, for even ordinations themselves would not escape the universal disaster. When the ordaining bishop comes gradually to reject the Church's faith in the Holy Sacrifice of the Mass; when, as a natural consequence, his intention is altered and no longer to ordain for the Holy Sacrifice, he will end up transforming the rite and will cease to confer the priestly character on the ordinands. His ordinations will be invalid. It was by a similar process that, in the sixteenth century, the Anglican bishops ceased to validly confer Holy Orders. Now, it lies in the very logic of collegiality to repeat this process, and indeed, to systematise and extend it.

Collegiality has everything needed to transform the faith and therefore destroy it, but nothing to preserve it. By practically stripping bishops of their personal power to transmit sound doctrine, by subjecting the bishops' faith to the perpetual revision of deliberating and voting assemblies, collegiality comes imperceptibly to transform the bishops' faith. Once their faith is changed, their intention in conferring the sacraments that fall under their power will likewise change. Change of rite will swiftly follow change of intention, and then the sacrament will be null.

The bishops who embraced Anglicanism under Edward VI in the sixteenth century had undoubtedly received valid consecration and genuinely possessed the power of Holy Orders. Nevertheless, from the moment they lost faith in the Holy Sacrifice of the Mass, changed their intention, and modified the rite, their once-real powers ceased to confer the true priesthood[8] This is unquestionably what would befall the collegialized bishops if the system is not soon reduced to rubble.

The powers of the Church, whether of jurisdiction and of Holy Orders, are personal powers. The Lord has established them thus once and for all, founding them in this manner because personal appointment accords with the sacred laws of frankness and honour. Therefore, let each minister know that it is he who is chosen, honoured to such a degree, and invested with this divine charge—he personally, not some anonymous collective.

---

[8] See, in *Dictionnaire de Théologie Catholique*, vol. 11.2 (Paris: Librairie Letouzey et Ané, 1932), "Ordinations anglicanes," § III, "Les arguments contre la validité" (cols. 1168ff., especially cols. 1183–1186).

Let each of those who turn to the Lord's ministers, sub-mitting to their powers, listening to their preaching, attend-ing their Masses, and participating in the Holy Sacrifice, feel secure. Let the ministers themselves feel secure, in relation to their brethren. No one should fear deception or be driven to the despairing confusion of questioning whom they encounter or what is at stake: the authentic, truly supernatural power of a minister of Christ, or the mere simulacrum of power of a faceless assembly?

Our Lord, having willed that powers in His Church be personally attributed and exercised, shall not permit col-legiality to absorb or suppress them. Rather, He will put an end to collegiality one way or another. We need not fear, therefore, but should pray with full confidence and unhesitatingly exercise, according to Tradition and within our sphere, the power that is ours, thereby preparing those happy times when Rome will remember to be Rome and bishops to be bishops.[9] For Rome shall regain her primacy and shall put an end to this collegial farce that permits bish-ops to commit schism as a national assembly, as an organized group, and collectively, while none among them dares to declare himself personally schismatic, quite the reverse. It will not take a century, nor even half a century, to put an end to this sort of irresponsible exchange that has multiplied since the Council:

"Your Excellency, how could you put up with what that reli-gious said in his talk on original sin and the infant baptism?"

---

[9] In *this brief apologia* we have only considered the first characteristic of collegiality, the depersonalization and hence annulation of powers. But we must take care not to forget the second characteristic, insepa-rable from the first and no less ruinous: the suppression of episcopal sovereignty. For, as Abbé Raymond Dulac has very aptly observed (*Courrier de Rome*, 10 January 1971), "episcopal collegiality tends to sunder sovereign power and divide its responsibilities between the one once known as the Sovereign Pontiff and the local churches."

"For my part, I wouldn't talk like that. But what can I do? How can I step in, when the French bishops' conference now thinks that we can't be sure about any of these things anymore?

"Your Excellency, how could you put up with that priest periodically gathering your diocese's clergy together to teach them what can only be called a mockery of the Holy Mass?"

"Personally, I don't like his theories or his approach. But look, he has either been granted authority, or has secured it, through the liturgical commission, and that commission is approved and encouraged by our episcopal conference. How do you expect me, all by myself among the bishops, to stand up against it? It's impossible."

But it would indeed be possible, if only the bishop possessed a modicum of priestly courage; if only he dared to face his duty squarely, to expose himself to contempt, mockery, and perhaps even social ostracism, in order to bear witness to the Sovereign Priest, Jesus Christ. Yet he has allowed himself to be caught in mechanisms deliberately designed to prevent him from being what he truly is, in legitimate submission to Rome. After this initial abdication of authority, where will he find the courage to confess the faith and combat heretics?

The first mistake was to enter into this Rousseauist-style collegial system, wherein the official holder of power is stripped of effective authority while retaining its façade. Yet this system will be torn asunder and all its mechanisms shattered. Certainly, specialized commissions will not be abolished. They have always been indispensable for the study of particularly arduous questions. But they will no longer function anonymously. It will be clear who appoints them, what their authority encompasses, and to whom their members must answer for their work. This includes meetings among bishops as well. These will not be suspended, since they are natural and do promote, to a certain extent, fervour in prayer and fruitful apostolic work. But let them be governed by clear statutes approved by Rome. Let each bishop be encouraged to take his duties more seriously, rather than be absorbed into a system that strips him of his powers and relieves him of responsibility for his ministry. In a word, let the collegialist and democratic Revolution end: the holiness of the Church and our own sanctification depend upon it.

Indeed, the holiness of the entire Church and the sanctification of each of her members do not require that we should never face the scandal of heresy in a bishop or in a doctor he has accredited. What it does require is that we can still appeal to the Chair of Peter against such heretics, that they do not become indistinguishable before Rome, slipping away and hiding in the opaque fog of collegiality.

Nor do the holiness of the entire Church and the sanctification of each of her members require that the scandal of invalid or sacrilegious Masses never arise, but that bishops who are guilty of or complicit in such enormities can no longer exploit the nearly infallible protection of collegial camouflage to pass for innocent and escape the justice of the Roman Pontiff. For whilst "it must needs be that scandals come,"[10] it is nonetheless necessary that the Church not be dominated by scandals, and therefore that her governance enable her to vanquish them and remain both holy and sanctifying. Such is precisely the effect of the governance wherewith Our Lord has endowed her thanks to those supernatural and hierarchical powers, assisted by the Holy Ghost and personally attributed.

---

[10] Matthew 18:6.

The post-Conciliar disorders in general, and perverse collegiality in particular, would have been contained and suppressed immediately had priests in large numbers possessed no other aspirations but to glorify the Sovereign Priest, treating with the utmost respect the ineffable powers He has entrusted to our hands. It should be enough for every priest, whether of the first or second order, to honour Him who consecrated us. It should be enough for us to act in all things as His faithful ministers,[11] and to do what lies within our powers so that He may find consolation and glory when it pleases Him to use us, whether as pure instruments in the Holy Sacrifice, as dispensers of His truth in preaching, or as lieutenants of His sovereignty in whatever exercise of jurisdiction may fall to our lot.

Priests and bishops who have come to a profound awareness that the Lord Himself deigns to use them to offer the Holy Mass are horrified at the very idea of polyvalent rites. Having given themselves to the Lord of all truth so that He may offer His Sacrifice through them, they shall under no circumstances and for no reason allow themselves to fail to conform, in so sacred a function, to faithful and unambiguous rites marked by the deepest reverence, preserved for us by Tradition. The incompatibility between the God of all truth and equivocal rites is absolute. To accomplish the mystery of faith—*Mysterium Fidei*—according to a rite that by its very nature destroys the faith is to mock the Lord with great insolence and horrible wickedness.

"O Lord," the faithful priest sighs inwardly, "O Lord, mayst Thou have the satisfaction of finding in me a worthy minister of the Holy Sacrifice that Thou art about

---

[11] "Here now it is required among the dispensers, that a man be found faithful" (1 Corinthians 4:2).

to offer through me, poor sinner that I am. Let me at least do this for Thee, to avoid grieving Thee when Thou deignest to employ me. And to avoid grieving Thee, to surrender myself wholly to Thine action with complete availability, what better course could I take than to begin by adhering to the most sacred rites, sanctioned by the Church of the ages?"

And for his part, will a bishop aware of the trust Jesus Christ places in him to shepherd a portion of His flock not implore the Sovereign and Eternal Pontiff that he may be, in all perfection, the living image of the Good Shepherd? Will he not implore that he might at least bear his office's duties at his own risk and peril, even unto death, rather than let irresponsible collegiality strip them away? Will he not implore that he may faithfully transmit the doctrine of the faith and, to that end, safeguard Catholic Tradition?

May all of us who, by the intercession of Our Lady Co-Redemptrix, have received a share in the ministerial priesthood possess the firmest resolution to honour the Sovereign Priest. Then shall our powers be exercised in perfect conformity to the institution of Our Lord and the Tradition of His Church, for the sanctification of the faithful, our own sanctification, and the greater splendour of the Holy City.

Obviously, it would be wholly erroneous to attempt to explain the supernatural in terms of sentimental love, or to misconstrue justification as a mere legal fiction, as Luther did. So too, it would be misguided to penetrate into the mystery of the Church through *analogies* drawn, perhaps unwittingly, from unnatural and revolutionary societies. Such societies, in varied ways, propose earthly messianism as an ideal to be attained and a common good to be realized, and establish their power through secret organizations and anonymous structures.

Not all analogies are suitable for reflection on just any supernatural mysteries, nor can every concept be employed to arrive at a certain understanding of the secrets revealed by God. For instance, understanding the holy humanity of Christ requires more than indiscriminately attributing to Him both the greatness and weaknesses of the human condition. Rather, one must recognize that the nature He deigns to assume cannot but *be filled with wisdom and grace*, and moreover, that the infirmities He chose to bear can never be the physical or psychological defects that arise from the loss of integrity following original sin.[12] Christ was subject to thirst, fatigue, certain sorrows, and the terrible torments of the Cross, but He was necessarily exempt from illness or psychological deficiencies. He could suffer from such evils only in the members of His Mystical Body.[13]

In a certain sense, the Church is like Christ Himself, since she is nothing other than "Jesus Christ poured forth and communicated."[14] To express the truth about her, one must understand that this society, sent from heaven, incorporates and elevates certain properties of a just society while remaining necessarily exempt from the artifices and flaws characteristic of revolutionary societies.

Now, the conception of the Church that is spreading today introduces a dangerous novelty: the transposition of the false and pernicious Rousseauist or Masonic idea of society. Many theologians, or those who pose as such, admire collegiality and applaud pseudo-messianic initiatives that parody the Gospel, because they find the

---

[12] See *Summa Theologiae*, III, q. 14, a. 4.
[13] See Blaise Pascal, "Prayer to Ask of God the Proper Use of Sickness," especially paragraph 10.
[14] Jacques-Bénigne Bossuet, "Letter on the Unity of the Church," trans. Hugh Farmer, *Life of the Spirit* 11, no. 127 (1957): 326.

revolutionary concept of society entirely natural. Hence, their theology of the Church has become aberrant.

Politics overturns their theology. In certain cases, faith itself—the content of the faith and the entirety of religion—founders, because it can no longer withstand the more or less conscious pressure of a political error that permeates the mind—an unbridled political passion driven by the relentless demands of a false messianism.

The mystery of the Church is then reduced not only to a mere worldly reality but, far worse, into an unnatural reality, a cerebral, devastating, and insatiable monster. It is against this radical distortion, this insidious perversion of the mystery of the Church, that we have reaffirmed the traditional doctrine of the *Sancta Civitas*.

6

The Church's Messianism

THE CHURCH'S POWERS FLOW from Christ's own, and her holiness is Christ's own "poured forth and communicated." Therefore, her messianism is the expression of the only true messianism, that of Christ Jesus, Our Lord and Our King. *Regnum meum non est de hoc mundo... Tu dicis quia Rex sum Ego.*[1] Free from anything nebulous, impure, utopian, or grasping, this messianism announces to men, and even brings to them here below, in a certain sense, liberation, renewal, and peace. Yet it is from sin that the Church delivers us by baptizing us into Christ's Passion, not necessarily from economic servitude or tyrannical oppression. "Unless a man be born again of water and the Holy Ghost, he cannot enter into the Kingdom of God."[2] "You seek me because you were filled. Labour not for the meat which perisheth, but for that which endureth unto life everlasting."[3]

---

[1] John 18:36–37. See the Gospel of the feast of Christ the King on the last Sunday of October, or the Passion according to Saint John on Good Friday. See also Appendix 5, "A Doctrinal Note on the Mystery of Christ the King."
[2] John 3:5.
[3] John 6:26–27.

Similarly, the peace which the Church bestows does not erase national boundaries, abolish the traditions proper to each country, or exempt states from safeguarding their legitimate interests. Her peace does not belong primarily to the temporal order, but rather to that of faith, charity, and common docility to a supernatural hierarchy. "Peter . . . I will give to thee the keys of the Kingdom of heaven."[4] "These things I have spoken to you, that in me you may have peace. In the world you shall have [much] distress; but have confidence, I have overcome the world."[5]

Three passages in the Gospel admirably express the intention and grand design of the Church's messianism. "Seek ye therefore first the kingdom of God, and his justice, and all these things shall be added unto you."[6] "But one thing is necessary. Mary hath chosen the best part, which shall not be taken away from her."[7] "I am a King, but my Kingdom is not from hence."[8]

The Church's messianism first distinguishes the spiritual from the temporal; secondly, it centres on the conversion of hearts and the life of grace; and finally, it demands consent to the Cross in both the temporal and the spiritual realms. Its purpose is by no means to supplant earthly kingdoms nor to fulfil the mission entrusted to them. However, insofar as these kingdoms receive this messianism, it causes a just political peace to flourish within them, a *pax Christiana*. This vale of tears undoubtedly remains a region of exile, trial, and struggle, but far from being, like the modern world, a foretaste of Gehenna with its dreadful cries and gnashing of teeth, the *vale of tears* becomes

---

[4] Matthew 16:19.
[5] John 16:33.
[6] Matthew 6:33.
[7] Luke 10:42.
[8] John 18:36–37

a habitable land. Infused with the purest sweetness, it allows one to anticipate, through one's tears, the eternal consolations of our heavenly homeland. Without ceasing to be the vale of tears, the earth becomes the land of the evangelical beatitudes.[9]

When these marks are lacking or are erased, a counterfeit messianism invades the world: a carnal and Judaic messianism, Masonic and Communist, of the devil and his minions. Men are beguiled by promises of liberty, communion, and peace, yet liberty is spurious when the human heart refuses to be moved by grace, for in that case it does not overcome the tyranny of pride and the passions. Likewise, communion is artificial when individuals and societies are withdrawn from the only powers capable of shattering selfishness and falsehood: the supernatural and hierarchical powers of the Church of Christ. As for peace, apart from divine love, it can only be the bleak result, under the direction of a totalitarian state, of the highly sophisticated workings of propaganda and police. It is the image of that accursed order which reigns in hell.

It is an unprecedented aberration, alas, that some churchmen have now indubitably become the heralds and purveyors of earthly messianisms. Consider this proclamation by the Cardinal-Archbishop of Paris: "Who has taken seriously the appeal of the Christian churches on behalf of the Third World during the second decade of development? Who has heeded the Pope's proposal at the United Nations to impose an international tax to bring justice to the oppressed of the earth? How many campaign for a policy of sharing and respect among all men?"[10]

---

[9] See our essay on the spiritual life, *Sur nos routes d'exil, les Béatitudes* (Paris: Nouvelles Éditions Latines, 1960).
[10] *La Croix*, 29–30 November 1970.

One could continue in the same vein and say equivalently, as so many "post-Conciliar" priests do: "Offended and humiliated men of all nations, unite in supra-religious internationals and build a free and fraternal humanity beyond all dogmas, all morals, and all rites! Believers of all religions and unbelievers of all sects, join together in a great international alliance of religious or irreligious opinions! The collective success of mankind: that is the god of the future."

What answer can be given to priests who have perverted the Gospel's language? Simply this: their gospel without grace is useless to mankind in promoting the development of our unhappy species along lines of non-Christian solidarity, indifferent to all faith.

O misguided priests who betray your priesthood! Know that peoples and nations do not need to hear you to pursue what you now proclaim. To organize comfort and security on a global scale as the highest objective and supreme law, no one shall turn to the ministers of Jesus Christ, to the priests of the *New and Eternal Testament*. That is not your mission. Freemasons and the Counter-Church will do a much better job. The Counter-Church might briefly thank you for bringing in a Catholic audience, but once that is done, it will do quite well without your services. You were not ordained for this.

The Church, as history attests, is not immune to false popes. Yet she is too holy, and the powers she holds from Christ are too divinely assisted, for her not to swiftly discern the true pope in times of great trial—one who condemns falsehood and strengthens the chain of continuity, however momentarily shaken.

While not immune to false popes, the Church is equally vulnerable to the possibility of being governed by an enigmatic pope whose actions might bear the mark of a false messiah. In the era of mediaeval or classical Christendom, such a possibility was scarcely conceived, for if any Sovereign Pontiff had taken it into his fancy to play the false messiah, he would have been promptly called to order and disabused of his delusions, so strongly would he have offended not only the interests of Christian princes but also their faith and common sense.

Behold us now in an age where Christendom lies in disarray. The temporal order is largely enslaved to institutions of lies, intrinsically perverse and opposed to both natural law and the Gospel. Moreover, bishops are increasingly selected according to criteria not incompatible with the anti-Christian Revolution, chosen to avoid conflict with unnatural political organizations and to avoid displeasing their overt or covert leaders. That is why one wonders what major obstacle would prevent the rise of a pope fascinated by false messianism.[11] Yet against the excesses of such a pope there remains the supreme and insurmountable barrier of the Holy Ghost's assistance. It is well understood that His assistance does not render the pope indefectible in every respect, but its effects are extraordinarily precious even in the most unfavourable cases, namely, guaranteeing infallibility and confining the Vicar of Christ's defectibility within strictly defined limits, ensuring that, whatever his faults, he does not impose formal heresy.

Here it is fitting to recall the common doctrine regarding the privileges of the papacy and their absolute necessity

---

[11] These considerations did not occur to Charles Cardinal Journet, who, when speaking of the papacy *betrayed by some of its custodians*, asserts that nowadays "this danger is abolished" because of the drastic reduction of the papacy's temporal possessions. The danger, however, has only changed its form. See *The Church of the Word Incarnate*, trans. Dominic Spiekermann, ed. Matthew K. Minerd, vol. 3, *The Catholic Unity of the Church* (Steubenville, Ohio: Emmaus Academic, 2025), 917.

for the life of the Church. "Fortunately, we have the pope, unlike the Protestants," a devout Christian lady, an ardent supporter of the new rites, once boldly remarked to me when I explained my rejection of polyvalent Masses. It would be impious to diminish her faith-filled words in any way, yet it is both useful and Christian to elucidate their meaning with precision.

"Fortunately, we have the pope," to safeguard doctrine and the sacraments; to shepherd Our Lord's entire flock, lambs and sheep, prelates and simple faithful alike; to guide and correct this flock through the infallible decisions of the extraordinary Magisterium or, more commonly, through acts of the ordinary Magisterium in continuity with Tradition.

"Fortunately, we have the pope," not to meditate on the mysteries of the faith in our stead, but so we may be enlightened and protected in our personal meditation on them through His teaching, which is assisted by God's Spirit; not to supplant the ministry of bishops and preachers, but to allow them to fulfil that ministry in truth, without error and without leading souls astray.

Although we sometimes endure bad popes who, to some degree, betray the Church and the papacy, their betrayal necessarily has limits, for they remain preserved from teaching formal heresy. Even with bad popes, Christians do not go astray when they follow those papal prescriptions that conform to the Church's Tradition, for in these, bad popes are not bad but good and beneficent.

"Fortunately, we have the pope," not to prevent us from opening our eyes by demanding blind obedience, nor to impose upon us a horrible distortion of obedience that refuses or neglects clear discernment; not to forbid us any resistance of an order's content or form; not to spare us every trial in obedience. Rather, the pope serves first to spare us the unbearable trial of lacking a visible, universal, and infallible Vicar in the very things of Christ; and second, to allow us to maintain peace even when our obedience is severely tested, for we must resist measures or orders that lead to sin, either because they oppose moral virtues or because they in some way oppose the faith itself, such as by neglecting to condemn heresies.

Resistance would disturb the peace only if the orders or measures requiring our refusal were simultaneously forbidden by God speaking through His natural or revealed law and imposed by God speaking through His Vicar. We would then face an insoluble conflict. But we are assured beforehand that this cannot happen. Indeed, when the pope commands or fails to condemn, when required, gravely culpable acts contrary either to morality or even, in some respects, to the safeguarding of the faith, he no longer acts as the Vicar of Christ. It is no longer Jesus Christ who speaks through him. To resist him then is not to resist Christ, but is rather to obey Christ. It is, moreover, to honour the dignity of the Vicar of Christ to refuse to yield a point where he dishonours that dignity. And, because we honour his dignity, our act of resistance paradoxically remains respectful and filial. To act thus is to remain in harmony with the Lord and with His Vicar among us, at least in matters that certainly pertain to the Lord. In this harmony lies our peace, even though resistance itself remains painful.

"Fortunately, we have the pope." When we recognize him for what he truly is and are devoutly docile to him, we secure Church's most magnificent treasures in our life and soul, especially true devotion to the Blessed Virgin and true worship of the Eucharist. Yet these treasures, proper to the Catholic Church, are infinitely above the pope who serves as their guardian. We do not place the

Blessed Virgin, the Eucharist, and the pope on the same level. Docility to the pope, however pious it may be, always implies the condition that the Blessed Sacrament is served first and that true devotion to Our Lady is maintained.[12]

Thus, even if some pope were to assume the guise of a false messiah,[13] it would only be fleeting, marked by hesitations and repentance. He would not fully or openly embrace his second role as the tempter of the Church and instrument of the devil. He would never proclaim, for example, as a settled teaching of the ordinary Magisterium, or as an authentic interpretation of twenty centuries of Catholicism, still less as an *ex cathedra* definition, that the *ascent of mankind* and its earthly success is now the new form of our religion. Rather, he would indistinguishably blend two messages fundamentally opposed in their very essence: on the one hand, the Promethean message of worldly domination, according to the Three Temptations and *practically* without regard for the sovereignty of God or the sinfulness of man; on the other hand, the message of the Christian faith which announces Redemption solely through the Cross of Our Lord Jesus Christ. This unnatural entanglement would surely push scandal to its ultimate limit, posing a dangerously seductive threat. Nevertheless, it could neither lead the elect astray nor destroy the Church. First, because Jesus' promise to Peter shall not fail: "I have prayed for thee, Peter, that thy faith fail not, and thou, being once converted, confirm thy brethren."[14]

---

[12] On these questions, see Charles Cardinal Journet, *Le Message Révélé* (Paris: Desclée de Brouwer, 1964), chapter 4. See also our articles "La certitude dans l'Église" in *Itinéraires* 145 (July-August 1970): 36–48 and "Sans mauvaise conscience" in *Itinéraires* 148 (July-August and December 1970): 8–22.

[13] See Appendix 3, "On the Church and the Pope."

[14] Luke 22:32

Second, we affirm the certain and universal principle that the order of good and that of evil are not opposed on equal terms nor symmetrical. This means, in particular, that the author of scandal shall always be but a creature, whereas the defender against scandal is the Almighty Lord Himself. The world's insinuations, propaganda, pressures, and persecutions, however much support they may receive from churchmen, are in no way comparable to the Lord's grace, whether as a force that penetrates freedom or as a sweetness that draws it to perfect love. Grace belongs to a different order than that of all created things, and is infinitely stronger than them.[15]

Finally, the Virgin Mary's maternal and royal intercession shall always defend the Church victoriously against the snares of false messianisms. Even if a pope were to lend some measure of assistance to those who have sworn to obtain the humanitarian transformation of the religion of Jesus Christ, the successor of Peter's dizzying complicity would be neutralized in advance and rendered ineffective by the supplication of Our Lady Co-Redemptrix. Was not her prayer for Peter's conversion already ascending—silent yet irresistible—while she stood at the foot of the Cross of her Son with the Beloved Disciple and the holy women, while the other apostles had shamefully fled, Peter among them? Could Jesus, who became man by Mary's *fiat*, fail to lend ear to the supplication of the Virgin His Mother? Could He fail to hear it as her Son, in an hour of darkness where this intercession would become, as never before, a matter of life or death for the Catholic Church?

> *Monstra te esse matrem*
> *Sumat per te preces*
> *Qui pro nobis natus*
> *Tulit esse tuus.*

---

[15] See *Mystères du Royaume de la Grâce*, vol. 1, p. 84ff.

False messianism will not prevail against the Church or against the papacy. The Church, founded upon Peter, shall unto the end preserve in her heart and spread among men the sole true messianism, that of Jesus Christ. His is a messianism of grace, conversion, and the Beatitudes. His is a messianism that resides in its fulness in the Kingdom that is not of this world, thus extending its influence over the kingdoms of this world, if they receive the law of the Gospel and strive to accomplish their temporal work *through the King of Heaven.*

EPILOGUE

IT IS USEFUL TO UNMASK THE MOD-
ernists' stratagems and reveal that these heretics lie
when they claim that they do not touch the Church,
but merely to assist her renewal and expansion. In reality,
they betray the Church and seek her destruction, because
they hypocritically tear away what is essential to her life
in order to substitute that which would lead to her death,
were it not for the divine promise that she will overcome
every disaster. Indeed, against the Church, mistress of
truth, they seek to impose a manner of expression and sort
of Magisterium that would transform her into a diabolical
pseudo-prophetess, dispensing to the world an endlessly
changing doctrine couched in vaguely Christian phrase-
ology. Against the Church that dispenses God's grace
through the seven sacraments and offers the Lord the
one true sacrifice, they seek to impose a different Missal
and ritual that would universalize sacramental invalidity
or sacrilege, transforming the liturgy into a pitiable pseudo-
religious spectacle.

The essential flaw of modernism is mendacity. These
men lie, and they would make the Church the perfect
institution of universal falsehood. To this end, they labour
to strip away what makes her truly herself, seeking to
deprive her of the indispensable and traditional means of
being the true Church.

Collegiality threatens the efficacy of the power of
jurisdiction and even the power of Holy Orders. *Ritual
changes* expose the Mass to invalidity. *Systematic aban-
donment of irreformable formulas* tears dogma to shreds.
Pseudo-messianism, finally, dissolves holiness into humanitarian fantasy.

The fact remains that modernism has plunged the Church into agony, and no meditation on the Church's nature, however pious and justificatory, suffices to meet the trial that overwhelms her. What is still urgently needed is to keep vigil beside the Lord Jesus who is in agony in His Church. "Jesus will be in agony even to the end of the world. We must not sleep during that time."[1] He shall be in agony in His Church until the end of the world, first in the sense that He shall continue to suffer in His afflicted members who, for love of Him, willingly embrace or at least do not refuse the torments of sickness, the persecutions of external enemies, and even the cruel renunciations that absolute fidelity to the law of grace demands. However, at certain particularly terrible periods—and we are in one of these periods—Jesus is in agony in His Church in another manner, which adds to the former. He is in agony because His Church is hindered, mocked, thwarted, and attacked from within in her primordial office as dispenser of Redemption. Not that she is near to disappearing, since the gates of hell shall not prevail; rather, her own sons, hierarchical leaders among them, mistreat her with such vile wickedness that she advances only to fall back with every step, exhausted and languishing.

Let us open our eyes and see. Although the traditional Mass has never been abolished, it is increasingly common for Mass to be celebrated ambiguously and profaned by sacrilege. Although the preaching of sound doctrine has never fallen silent, false prophets and lying theologians often render it uncertain. Likewise, although holiness remains ever-flowing and pure, it is not uncommon for it to be parodied and caricaturized with the vilest counterfeits. Such is one of the forms Our Lord's agony takes within

---

[1] Pascal, *Pensées*, 552 in Brunschvicg's numbering, trans. Trotter, 176.

the Church in our day. "We must not sleep during that time." But how are we to watch and keep Him company?

First, let us redouble our prayers with peace and love. Then, recognizing that participating in Church life is now impossible without exposing ourselves to all manner of trouble, let us not shrink back from this suffering but endure it in union with the Church, herself suffering and overwhelmed. Some examples: We must persevere in the study of Holy Writ at all costs, even in the face of myriad obstacles that prevent us from examining and nourishing ourselves thence. We must not hesitate to take pains in wisely assisting those priests who celebrate the Mass of the ages. Similarly, we must not hesitate, despite the humiliations that might await us, to raise our respectful yet persistent appeals to ecclesiastical authorities—which often mock us—to restore to us *Scripture, the Catechism, and the Mass.* We must above all take care to seek within this holy Church that modernists would de-spiritualize, the means she will never lack to preserve the primacy of prayer and contemplation.

These examples offer us a glimpse of what it means to watch with Jesus who is in agony within the Church. We shall succeed in watching only because He shall make us capable of it through His very Church. Far from saying that we suffer because of the Church, we should rather say that we suffer with the Church, in union with her, thanks to the divine succour the Church continues to bestow upon us from the depths of her distress.

By remaining more united than ever to the Church in this exceptionally cruel situation, we confess our faith in the Church. This vigil during her agony constitutes, in these times of bloodless persecution, the form our confession of faith must take. Let us examine its particular characteristics more closely.

Modernism does not attack head-on but from beneath, insidiously introducing equivocation everywhere. Hence, to confess the faith before modernist authorities is to reject every equivocation in both rite and doctrine. It means adhering to Tradition because it remains clear, honest, and irreproachable both in dogmatic definitions and ritual order.

Regarding the rites of the Mass specifically, let us clearly recognize that one cannot confess the Church's faith within the Mass nor categorically repudiate deadly modernist ambiguity except by adhering to the traditional rite—over a millennium old—which offers no opening to heresy. Accepting the new rites, even with genuine piety and orthodox preaching about the Mass, would assuredly not constitute an uncompromising confession of faith or adequate repudiation of heresy in its present form. The very concession of accepting the new polyvalent celebration, puts us on a path of practical denial. What then can verbal declarations or pious gestures accomplish? They become merely contradictions compounding equivocation.

Faced with authorities seeking to impose falsehood in its worst form—the modernist form—and amidst a Christian people bewildered by this unprecedented imposture, it becomes immediately clear that fully to confess the faith in the Church that preserves the true Mass is, above all, to continue to celebrate the Mass of the ages. While this certainly brings suffering, the Church whose true Mass we celebrate grants us, by that very act, the grace to bear such suffering with courage and ease.

Preserving teaching and rites *intact* does not mean petrified immobility and dead routine, but rather an ordered and living permanence. In a time of Revolution, *to preserve intact* means not undertaking wholesale adaptations, for the obvious reason that the authority which presides over the whole either does not exist or has become complicit in the disorder. We must limit ourselves to adaptations limited within our small sphere of real authority. Within these bounds, however, our fervent and wise attachment to Tradition, should make us unafraid to implement the adaptations that the very life of Tradition requires.

Even in a time of liturgical Revolution, for example, faithfully maintaining not only Latin, but the Latin texts before Paul VI, must not keep us from paying attention to the diversity of Christian assemblies seeking to participate in liturgical worship. In a time of Revolution, keeping Tradition intact does not mean refusing to live, but living in order—in the order of our little stronghold, maintaining contact with the neighbouring strongholds—since the whole land suffers systematic anarchy. To live in order, even within narrow confines, is the complete opposite of slumbering, grumbling idly, or consuming oneself with impotent rage and disgust. It means doing, within the limits the Revolution imposes on us, the utmost possible to live in Tradition with intelligence and fervour. *Vigilate et orate.*

APPENDICES

I Believe in Holy Church

THE CURRENT TRIAL AFFLICTING the Church is profound and universal. It has reached the point that prelates and theologians, who until quite recently were incredibly optimistic, now betray a certain unease in their conversations, lectures, and articles. Doubtless the Church, born from the pierced side of Jesus on the Cross and assisted by the Holy Ghost, cannot be destroyed. Neither miseries of the times, the frailties of men, nor the fury of the devil can prevent her, even today, from bringing forth saints in every condition of life. We may well have tangible evidence of this extraordinary wonder. Yet this trial penetrates to the very depths of our souls. It wounds and bruises us. Faith, courage, and the resolve to persevere in the tradition received from the Apostles do not suffice to alleviate the pain, or at times, the anguish. Under these circumstances, I ask the reader's indulgence if I begin *ex abrupto*.

Let those misguided clerics, then, muster the courage to express openly what they now insinuate with such reluctance. Let them boldly proclaim, if they dare, let them recite and sing an updated Creed, saying: I believe in a mutable Church, which must make up for her tardiness in keeping up with history and convert from her sins. As for us, firmly rooted in two millennia of tradition, we continue to believe in Holy Church, eternally one across all ages, free from faults and without need of conversion, tirelessly fostering the conversion of those she has begotten to supernatural life, never tardy in bringing salvation to sinners. This Church is not swayed by the currents of history, but by the Spirit of God (history is an occasion, not an efficient cause).

Let those deluded clerics, who have never shouldered the weight of any ecclesiastical institution—parish or monastery, independent school or orphanage—let those clerics, bereft of experience and untested by the trials of genuine reform, feverishly draft their simplistic yet convoluted, if not heretical, plans for "renewals," reorganizations, revisions, and modernizations on paper that tolerates all. As for us, we continue to hold that true and holy reformers first reform themselves, respect the heritage of the ages incorporated into the Church's treasury, and truly bear the burden of souls in order to meet their spiritual needs—needs that remain the same in essence, though some may be felt more keenly in one age than another.

At times, Christians who once lamented sclerosis and abuse now find themselves bewildered by reforms riddled with subversion, like an organ consumed by a devouring cancer. Will they lose their footing and succumb to the vertigo of doubt, or even of despair? Rather, let them—and us alongside them—recover courage and confidence by reaffirming our faith in the holy and indefectible Church. Let us remember that she possesses all that is needed to shield us today from false reforms, just as she defended us yesterday from sclerosis and routine. She did indeed defend us from them, but our hearts were not always pure enough to perceive it.

The Church's protection, today as yesterday, will become efficacious for us if we strive first for interior reform, if we lovingly preserve the inalienable deposit transmitted to us.

We all know, alas, the radical changes that subversion has been striving to impose upon us, especially since the Council. Let us consider a few examples. *In the dogmatic sphere*, the upheaval proceeds along two lines: either replacing defined and irreformable formulas with loose and flaccid expressions that harbour heresy, or maintaining a systematic silence concerning certain dogmas, such as original sin, the virginal motherhood of Our Lady, and the intrinsically supernatural character of the Kingdom of God.

In the liturgy, there is a calculated and insidious shift[1] that introduced a form of the celebration of the Mass that increasingly disregards the reality of the Holy Sacrifice, the Real Presence of the Body and Blood of Our Lord under the sacred species, and the role of the ministerial priest, which is in no way commensurate with that of the ordinary faithful. When pressed for reasons behind these dogmatic and liturgical changes, its proponents offer a series of arguments. (Their logical conclusion, though it may not be pursued to such an extreme, would be *the outright abolition of faith in the Church*.) They variously invoke the requirements of pastoral care, the demands of history and "modern man," and the "return to the Gospels."

Here is what ought to be answered, based on the article of the Creed: *et unam, sanctam, catholicam et apostolicam Ecclesiam.* Would it remain the same Church if, for *pastoral* reasons, she no longer gives souls the same truth across the ages, or made them participate in a different form of

---

[1] Proofs furnished in "Vers une liturgie carrément hérétique" in *Itinéraires* 118 (December 1967), p. 307.

worship, as though souls were no longer to be enlightened by the same dogmas, sanctified by the same rites, or drawn back to God by the same conversion? How could one still regard as the Bride of Christ and the living depositary of His truth a Church that "puts darkness for light, and light for darkness"?[2] A Church that in the time of Saint Athanasius proclaimed that Christ is consubstantial with the Father, yet in the time of Paul VI acquiesces to claims that He is only of the same nature, akin to children according to human generation, who are indeed of the same nature as their father, but form substances distinct from him?

Well then, if to legitimate the changes they have tried to introduce, they have recourse to the *demands of history*, I should ask: who is then the guide and inspirator of the Church: the future of humanity or the Holy Ghost given to the apostles on the day of Pentecost? Granted, in His infallible assistance, the Holy Ghost keeps in mind the vicissitudes of our history. No one dreams of denying that, for example, He raised up new missionary orders upon the discovery of the New World, as is fitting, because the fruitful action of the Holy Ghost is promised for all ages. Yet this is an action that enables the Church to transcend the ages, judge them, and answer the cries of souls from on high. It stands in stark contrast to an impulse that merges with humanity's flow, dissolves into ideologies and events, eschews all forms of condemnation, and hastens toward a so-called "building of the earth."

With regard to the "post-Conciliar" liturgical upheavals, they are not always imposed because of the demands of history, they are, rather, driven by a pastoral approach I have already critiqued, or by a "return to the Gospels." I then ask: What is a Church that, in order to rediscover

---

[2] Isaias 5:20.

Gospel's, deems it permissible to discard twelve or fifteen centuries of homogeneous development? Such a "return to the Gospels," in absolute discontinuity and negation, surely implies that the supernatural society founded by the Lord is not one and definitive, and capable only of homogeneous and harmonious growth.

This supernatural society therefore has no need to question the essential features of her worship. Unless she were to deny herself—which is unthinkable—the Church cannot, whatever the precautions,[3] alter a celebration of the Mass that admirably expresses and safeguards our unchanging faith in the sacrifice of our altars.

Let us recall here the indissoluble link that exists between Gospel renewal and ecclesiastical development. To clarify, I offer a personal allusion as a priest, and a Dominican priest. If I wish to return to the Gospels, must I discard the white habit our holy founder chose, break the rosary which added to our habit around the fifteenth century, and put on the attire of a travelling salesman or a stockbroker? Must I also give up preaching inside churches, especially when they are beautiful monuments,[4]

---

[3] Here is a fine example of *precaution* in the "post-Conciliar" liturgical overhaul: "One must certainly not unduly modernize inspired texts [in the translation for the liturgy in French] . . . Is it necessary, however, to *respect every editorial detail when they present pastoral inconveniences* and do not contribute to a deeper understanding of the text? . . . Let us keep all the trumpets of the Bible when they form part of a whole that explains them, *but let us consign to the props department without regret those which, for the public at our funerals, serve only to present the Word of God in an archaic and obscure language*" (Father Aimon-Marie Roguet, "Adieux à la trompette," in *La Vie Spirituelle* 544 [December 1967], pp. 594–595).

[4] On this matter, this is the stance of Father Yves Congar:

And in their desire "to be united to others with a view to Jesus Christ," [many clerics] feel uneasy about certain forms of the Church's "set-apartness": the habit, which not only sets one apart, but isolates and renders one strange; dwelling and instead deliver speeches at employment agencies or movie theatres?

Moreover, if I wish to be "Gospel-centred," must my speeches systematically reject dogmatic formulas like *original sin, virginal motherhood, and redemption from sin?* Must I question the distinct identity of my Order? Must a true return to the Gospels demand a break with our theological, disciplinary, and liturgical heritage that, while not explicitly detailed in the four evangelists' texts, exists there in germ, *destined to unfold harmoniously across centuries?*[5]

It is therefore inadmissible to attempt a return to the Gospels as though the Church were not a society that has grown and expressed itself in uniform institutions as soon as she enjoyed freedom as a society. The developments she has established and consecrated in dogmatic definitions, as well as the major points of canonical legislation, are not open to question. The Church has grown as

---

and way of life; vocabulary—or better, since it encompasses more— language, which belongs to a different world than that of men. Are these necessary? Does the faith demand them? Some even question whether we should have distinct church buildings at all. They are not merely questioning their monumental and prestigious character, *which we would agree to criticize with them,* but the very existence of a space "set apart," at least beyond its functional use on Sundays. On this point, we would disagree. We think the question touches something fundamental: the Church's "set-apartness," even as a dogmatic affirmation, and the role of the Church's visibility as a sign of the Kingdom that is not of this world.

We can already see that the question of worker-priests, as it actually arose, falls within the perspective we have just outlined ... Have not certain historical forms—contingent and relative—been confused with the essential? This is a question that shall one day be clarified. ("Église et Monde," in *Esprit* [February 1965]: 351–352.)

[5] Let us recall the parables of the mustard grain, the leaven, and the seed, and reread the passages about the action of the Holy Ghost in the discourse after the Last Supper.

she had the capacity and the duty to do according to the
Gospels themselves. Attempting to diminish or stunt this
growth in the name of rediscovering the Gospels would
be contrary to the Gospels themselves. Far from contra-
dicting the Gospels, the Church's natural and harmonious
development fulfils them in all truth. It is superfluous to
declare that these developments give rise to abuses and
accretions, for the Church never ceases correcting such
abuses (besides, I should like to know whether there exists
any institution in our *vale of tears* that men do not sooner
or later encumber and burden).

Therefore, these harmonious developments do not
contradict the Gospel, nor are they merely contingent
achievements subject to change according to time and
place. They are necessary to the Church and in harmony
with her nature. Persecutors who hate her and sons who
betray her may try to suppress them, but as soon as the
Church regains a measure of freedom, she restores and
revitalizes them. Thus, for example, as soon as the storm
of the French Revolution had slightly abated, the Church
reopened her convents, restored distinctive monastic habits, founded Catholic universities, built schools and hos-
pitals, rang the bells anew, and resumed public Eucharistic processions. The Church did so because she lives
the Gospel, and ecclesiastical development is the natural
effect of doing so.

It would be absurd to seek a return to the Gospels by
drying up the river, for the source cannot but become a
river. The perceived conflict between the source's purity
and the river's torrential abundance, between the Gospel's
simplicity and the Church's development in discipline,
worship, and doctrine, is illusory and harmful. The Gospel's simplicity remains present and radiant within this
vast development. When that simplicity is threatened, the

Church is always able to safeguard it, not by an impossible amputation, but through renewed fervour and purification that condemns false doctrines and represses abuses. In a word, by true reform. For true reforms do not oppose development; they preserve purity within development itself.

A widening rupture—evident in schisms and disorders—is dividing those who believe in the Church of the ages and those who, willy nilly, have accepted the revision of the Creed's article concerning the Church. The debate is not primarily about pastoral care, nor about "modern man," historical development, or even a "return to the Gospels." In reality, it is faith in the Church that lies at the heart of the present quarrel.

Some, including ourselves, thanks be to God, steadfastly believe that the Church was founded by Our Lord and that she has enriched herself by marvelous developments, especially when she has been able *to flourish* as a perfect society, the Holy Catholic, Apostolic, and Roman Church. Whatever the era, including our own, she has never failed in her mission, has kept inviolate the purity of her Gospel source, and has fulfilled her pastoral charge in adaptive, manifest, and fruitful ways.

Other Christians, however, have begun to doubt the perfection proper to the Church. They see evidence of her deficiencies and incapabilities in every domain. To remedy this, they advocate for transformations without a clear endpoint, guided only by the ever-shifting demands of the happier world they seek to create. In reality, they do not believe in a Church that stands free and independent of history, transcending and judging the world in order to save it. They view history as imposing itself on the Church, dominating and transforming her.

Critics argue that the traditional understanding of the Church as a holy and perfect society transcending history must be rejected because it would paralyze all reform. They contend the only valid perspective is that of a Church subject to the "demands of history." Yet, if this were true, how is it that the reforms worthy of the name—the only ones that have not betrayed the Church—have occurred not by yielding to the "demands" of history, but through the authority and sanctity that draw their standards from eternity rather than the passing hour?

This is not to say that all reforms have been initiated by saints. The Fathers of the Council of Trent, a reforming council if ever there was one, were very far from being all candidates for canonization. Nevertheless, that Council deserves the title of "holy" because it was legitimately convened and approved in the Holy Ghost, and its reforming decrees were implemented thanks to the inspiration and trials of saints. It is therefore entirely valid to assert that true reforms in the Church, although promulgated by legitimate authority, are a fruit of sanctity.

The reformers whom the Church has recognized and approved—Saint Bernard, Saint Dominic, Saint Catherine of Siena, or Saint John of the Cross—sought above all, with docility to legitimate authority, personal conversion and fidelity to the truth of the faith. Their actions were never driven by docility to the expectations of the world or the "demands of history."

In examining councils and reforms, one must certainly distinguish between personal conversion and the reform of abuses, but it is no less important to grasp the link between the two. Thus, in the case of the Council of Trent, the reform of abuses was achieved only thanks to the virtue of a few great saints and to the interior amendment of many of the faithful. Similarly, in our own time, the false reforms some seek to impose in the wake of the most recent council cannot be countered without a deliberate commitment to personal conversion. Without such conversion, how could one withstand the scandal of certain failures of authority, or the tenacious and perfidious pressures of an ersatz Church? Moreover, personal reform is the primary means—albeit not the only one—for paving the way for the condemnation of errors, the unmasking and removal of parallel authorities, and the implementation of true tradition on a sufficiently large scale and in full light of day.

Regarding reforms and the holiness of the Church, it is often observed that holy reformers were abruptly halted in their wise and necessary attempts to correct certain abusive customs or to rejuvenate some sclerotic organ of the Church. I am not unaware of this misfortune; indeed, I see an even more lamentable misfortune when reforms, which were about to be effected in a traditional sense, are thwarted by mediocre or jealous churchmen, only to be shortly thereafter seized and spoiled by veritable revolutionaries.

All this is incontestable. But what conclusion should be drawn? Should we put the Church herself on trial, reproaching her for having fallen short of her divine mission, or for having disappointing souls? On the contrary, does not justice demand that one recognize that these iniquities are not the Church's fault, but were committed in spite of her, against her law and her inspiration? In these misfortunes, what belongs to the Church—her truth, her wisdom, and her holiness—is not the jealousy, mediocrity, or treachery of those poor churchmen who fought against the holy reformers. Rather, it is, first, the zeal, patience, and humility of those reformers themselves, and then the conversion (when it comes) of their slanderers and enemies. In this alone is the Church revealed, together with the charity which animates her, the truth she dispenses, and the sanctifying effect of her hierarchical powers.

Furthermore, have those who reproach the Church for delays or sloth in the work of salvation really considered the deadly weight of their argument? Their reasoning ultimately gives the faithful and clergy who suffer under unjust ecclesiastical authorities plausible grounds for breaking with the Church. When a humble vicar, parish priest, or religious superior is struck by an absurd or iniquitous measure from above, what recourse remains to him, *if he has taken these theorists at their word*? The practical conclusions follow inexorably, leading straight to apostasy: "All that is happening to me is the Church's fault. There is nothing to hope for from a society that calls itself holy and apostolic yet is governed by prelates so unworthy of the saints and the apostles. Nothing remains but to get out of it, and quickly."

It becomes entirely logical to leave the Church when, having experienced certain hierarchs' lack of understanding of the needs of souls or of the spirit of the Gospel, one lays the blame for these shortcomings and faults upon the Church herself. The reason for remaining in the Church, whatever our sins and those of our brethren, and the reason for winning souls to her and retaining them in her fold, is that the Church is, in Bossuet's imperishable phrase, purely and simply "Jesus Christ poured forth and communicated." If the Church is *also* ignorance, malice, and saccharine falsehood poured forth and communicated, then what are we still doing in her communion? Why work to extend a religious society that, all things considered, is no better or worse than any other? Let the Muslims keep their Islam, the animists their animism, and the Buddhists their Buddha, since, in the end, the religion we would wish to bring them would also, sooner or later, fall far short of its task and fail in its mission. If the Church herself were the obstacle to sanctification and reform, or if she failed to act in time to save perishing souls, she would not be the supernatural, holy, and definitive society founded by the Son of God our Redeemer. In that case, one should seek a better-conceived and more fitting religious society, if indeed such a thing exists.

It would be inappropriate to argue that the Church's moral and "historical" failings ought not to turn us away from her, any more than the shortcomings and failings of any other society prevent its members from remaining in it. This argument fails because the Church is not just another society. She claims a unique status, incomparable to any other: *the dwelling of God among men, the Bride of Jesus Christ*, and nothing less. She claims the astonishing prerogative of fulfilling man's aspirations to the absolute, or rather of delivering supernatural goods, and justifying and sanctifying us through her divine powers. The Church, in a word, presents herself as a society of the order of grace: "Jesus Christ poured forth and communicated." Now, if at times this society deceives us, we lose assurance of finding in her the divine goods she promises. To remain within her is to risk complicity in an imposture. Thus, to condemn the Church as a sinful and prevaricating society while persevering in her as though she were holy and the infallible messenger of sanctification is a contradictory and logically untenable stance.

For our part, returning to Cardinal Journet's classical themes,[6] we affirm the mystery of the Church in the following terms. The Church does not sin. She asks pardon of the Lord *not for the sins she has committed*, but for the sins committed by her children, insofar as they fail to listen to her as their mother. The Church is not impure. *She purifies herself not in the sense of washing away her*

---

[6] See *The Church of the Word Incarnate*, trans. Spiekermann, vol. 3, 991–995.

own defilements, but in the sense that she purifies the children she has begotten, or in the sense that she grows in holiness, proceeding not from impurity but from a prior holiness. The Church is never deformed. *She reforms not in the sense that she recovers a doctrine she allowed to be corrupted, nor in the sense that she corrects her culpable habits*, but in the sense that she does not cease to bring her children back to the fullness of doctrine, uprightness of morals, and the sense of nobility and dignity in the exercise of their offices. The Church is never behind in her mission. If one must insist on saying that she "keeps pace with the age," this must be understood *not in the sense that she once lost time and, in certain periods, failed to present to the world the immutable truth and definitive salvation* so desperately needed in every century, but in the sense that she gives her children, in all ages, the ability to respond to souls' distress with pure compassion. In every age, the Church raises up countless Christians, clerics and laity, who understand the anguished cry of their mother: *quid fient peccatores* (what shall become of the sinners)?

The Church has no new doctrine to learn nor new means of salvation to discover. Yet she progresses in doctrine and in charity, *in the sense that the same content of the faith—unchangingly the same—is better explicated, and also in the sense that the fructification of grace is multiform, as varied as each of the elect and each great spiritual family*.

Such is our faith in the Church: one and holy, without stain or wrinkle, without slowness or ageing, without approximation or deficiency, without complicity in error or accommodation to sin, without naïveté or folly in the face of captious sophisms, or the hidden machinations of a false Church, of an *ersatz Church*.

The Church we believe in is ever ready for each moment of the time of Salvation, invulnerable to the errors and sins of the world and boundless in her mercy for souls who turn to her. Her face and heart retain unaltered the likeness of Our Lady, the Virgin Mother of God, who is her refuge, her mother, and her queen.

In this time of disarray, what is to be done? Above all, persevere in the faith handed down to us, *with its definitions and its anathemas.* One may promote reforms, but if one no longer regards the defined dogmas or the condemnation of errors, as if the world were to cease being the world, these reforms no longer deserve their name. They become subversive movements.

What else is to be done? By holding fast to the faith of the ages, let us strive to convert ourselves. Let us *do penance,* for the Kingdom of God—that is, Holy Church— *has truly come and is always in our midst.* "*Seek ye first the Kingdom of God and His righteousness,*" *and the rest, notably the strength to persevere,* "*shall be added unto us*" *as an additional gift.*[7]

Finally, a third attitude in the face of a reform that has fallen into the hands of subversion: maintain a living fidelity to the Church's age-old inheritance. Some advocate for a return, by virtue of a "Gospel *ressourcement,*" to forms of Christian life not yet fully explicated. This programme would abolish dogmatic formulations, strictly codified discipline, the ascetical state of life of the clergy, Gregorian chant, a particular liturgical language, and the Church's rights in civil society. This so-called return to a "true Gospel source," however, ignores the living tradition that flows from it. Such an interpretation of the Gospel is absurd, for it begins by rejecting the developments which proceed from it. For example, under the pretext of recovering the worship "in spirit and in truth" Christ promised

---

[7] Matthew 6:33

to the Samaritan woman, some reject the form of Catholic worship that began to become fixed in the fifth century, as if the innumerable host of holy priests who celebrated Mass according to the Canon failed to offer the Lord worship "in spirit and in truth."[8]

This type of *ressourcement* has a name: Protestantism. It is the Gospel without the Church, or more precisely, an arbitrary interpretation of the Gospel that seeks to ignore the Church, her growth, her inheritance, and her legislation. On the contrary, true *ressourcement*, if we must use the term, piously receives the Church's inheritance, removes, if need be, deforming superfluities and restores it to its finest expression, in accordance with tradition and not by virtue of the "demands of history." We have remarkable signs of this living fidelity to the Gospel source, ever flowing within a growing Church. Consider disciplinary documents such as Saint Pius X's *Motu Proprio* on sacred music at the dawn of the century, and, more recently, John XXIII's *Veterum Sapientia* on the Latin language.

Saintly reformers, the only ones to whom we remain attached, all proceeded in the same manner. Whether they reformed an Order, a country's clergy, or Church government, they all sought, first and foremost, their own personal reform. Then, in accordance with the legitimate Magisterium, they pronounced anathema upon the world, its false maxims, and its institutionalized scandals. Finally, they preserved, in living fidelity, the sacred inheritance of a Church that has grown according to the Gospel, from her first steps in Judaea and Samaria through the first recognition of her rights and privileges following the great Roman persecutions.

The type of reform now proposed for the Church can only bring terrible damage, because it is rooted in false

---

[8] John 4:24

principles. It presupposes either that the Church, with her disciplinary, dogmatic, and liturgical developments, has drifted away from the Gospel over the centuries, or that she is guilty of sin, especially sloth and delay, in bringing heavenly goods to the world. These presuppositions in turn derive from a very deficient faith in the Church, one that is weakened and debased, failing to grasp the supernatural elevation and purity of her mystery. Yet the Church is a truly supernatural society, truly holy, the *Mystical Body* of Christ, the unfailingly faithful Bride of Christ, in the image of the Virgin Mary. She is, across the centuries, without exception, until the end of the world, "Jesus Christ poured forth and communicated." This and nothing else.

Sons of the Church in a Time of Trial

I T WOULD BE FUTILE TO ATTEMPT to conceal from ourselves that the Church is being subjected by her Lord to a most severe trial, one of quite a novel character, for the enemies waging war against her are concealed within her very bosom. Despite frequently optimistic speeches, the current pope[1] has openly acknowledged this crisis; the very term "self-demolition" is his own. Daily experience confirms that neither the authority of the hierarchy nor the faith of the faithful function as it did before the Council. Jacques Maritain's phrase from *Le Paysan de la Garonne*, "immanent apostasy," rings truer each day with chilling precision. The evidence is overwhelming, revealing in palpable fashion the deficiencies of hierarchical authority, the alarming power of parallel authorities, liturgical sacrilege, and the heresies in doctrinal instruction.

In the face of this trial, many priests and faithful have taken the side of what they call obedience. Yet their actions do not reflect true obedience, for there are no

---

[1] Editor's note (1987): This article was written in 1975.

genuine commands offering full legal guarantees. Consider the cases with which I am well acquainted: religious men and women and secular priests. Some adopt secular dress, some recite a breviary devised by or for a single house, and priests—and I mean devout priests—compose liturgies that suit them better according to the times and the assemblies. Can one truly say that they obey? In reality, they follow ambiguous instructions, generally with little enthusiasm, passively accepting or "absorbing" innovations. The wisest among them hedge their bets, neither fully rejecting centuries-old practice nor fully embracing avant-garde positions. Even when they lean toward innovations, their actions do not constitute obedience in the true sense, for they lack conformity to clear, binding precepts. It seems above all[2] that they neither wish nor dare to oppose a certain trend whose value and validity they regard with some perplexity.

In any event, these priests, religious, and faithful remain resolved not to question the faith of the Church, nor the morality she teaches. We believe that, for a number among them, their docility and good faith have been caught off guard. They are deceived rather than culpable. Yet it has never occurred to us to think that they are no longer within the bosom of the Church. We consider them, naturally, as sons of the Church. The tragedy, the great tragedy, is that even unintentionally, their behaviour serves the cause of subversion. They have yielded to disastrous innovations—ambiguous, multifaceted changes introduced by hidden enemies—whose sole effect is to undermine solid tradition, weaken it, and ultimately, without awakening notice, change religion bit by bit. Under the guise

---

[2] We are speaking of simple regular and secular priests. The case of bishops and cardinals, especially in France and Rome, is certainly much more complex and troubling.

of necessary reforms and the pretext of trying to win over the Protestants, the Modernists, those covert heretics, have ushered in Revolution.

There are laymen, secular and regular priests, nuns, and—rarely—bishops, who, having discerned with varying speed and depth that the innumerable innovations proceed from the revolutionary intent of enemies working within the very sanctuary, have decided, out of attachment to the Church, to preserve what was practised and taught before this bitter and perilous period of *self-destruction.*

In the case of the Mass, they adhere to the rite, language, and texts of the *traditional Catholic Mass, Latin and Gregorian.* If they are bound to recite the Breviary, they still use the one universally employed before John XXIII. For the psalms, they use the millennial version prior to the ridiculous revision of Cardinal Bea's Jesuits.[3] They continue to say the Our Father and Hail Mary as they were taught. They still wear either the cassock of their clerical state or the habit of their religious profession. They teach the Catechism of Saint Pius X. In preaching, they do not confuse the life of grace with economic progress, and in their doctrinal study, they do not allow themselves to be misled by the chimera of attempting to reconcile the teachings of the Church with modern philosophies. Finally, they hold that, in the social and political order, the Church approves and favours only a city that conforms to natural morality and recognizes the rights of God

---

[3] This version, introduced at the close of Pius XII's pontificate, finds no defender today, not even in the Society of Jesus. To grasp the audacity of this *revision* of the psalter, with its abolition of Biblical Latin, one may consult the article "Versions de la Bible" in the *Dictionnaire de Théologie Catholique,* vol. 15.2 (Paris: Librairie Letouzey et Ané, 1950), cols. 2700–2739. But who, nearly thirty years ago, was interested in advising that great pope toward a "reform" so wholly at odds with tradition?

and of His Christ. They are certain that the Church does
not, and will never, place on equal footing a revolutionary
society and laws and a society conforming to natural and
Christian law. The Church condemns the Revolution and
will always condemn it, regardless of whether it is called
liberalism or socialism.

Well then! Can we accuse Christians who, aware of the
ambiguity of recent innovations as well as the perverse
intentions behind them, reject them out of attachment to
the faith and the Church, of disobedience? Should we
bemoan their blindness, reproaching them for indulging in
private judgement or setting themselves up as arbiters of
the situation? Should we be scandalized that they have no
guilty conscience? On the contrary, we must understand
that in the face of the lamentable absence of authority,
the alarming uncertainty of directives, and the bewilder-
ing array of changes, these faithful are not acting as self-
appointed judges. Rather, they cling to the settled body
of laws and customs preserved until John XXIII, which
were still peacefully received a mere fifteen years ago, and
which are altogether reliable, sustained by the force of tradition *in eodem sensu et eadem sententia*.[4]

The Christians I speak of pray with their whole
heart to Christ Our Lord, our chief and invisible King,
beseeching Him to manifest the power and holiness of
His governance over the mystical body through a visible
head, a Roman pontiff who, rather than lamenting self-
destruction, discharges his supreme office with clarity
and gentleness, confirming tradition, allowing for necessary adaptations, and doing so without ambiguity, safeguarding the essential from ruin. Until that day arrives,

---

[4] "In the same sense and meaning" (Saint Vincent of Lérins, *Commonitorium*). This passage was cited at the First Vatican Council,
constitution *De Fide Catholica*, at the end of chapter 4.

there is no justification for any Christian to accuse the faithful or priests who preserve tradition of disobedience. Far less is there any grounds for accusing them of no longer being sons of the Church.

The position of these faithful is far from easy. They refuse to make compromises or to collaborate with a clearly Modernist Revolution. In society, they are sidelined. Whatever their abilities, they are denied any positions of real responsibility. They do not complain, aware that they cannot bear witness without being exposed to criticism, suspicion, or exclusion to varying degrees depending on the place and people. They do not begrudge paying this price in order to remain true sons of the Church. If you hesitate to follow them, at least do not cast stones at them. You would be all the less justified in doing so, as they themselves have never considered condemning you, even though they believe that, perhaps without fully realizing it, you are playing into the hands of subversion.

These Christians who preserve tradition by conceding nothing to the Revolution ardently desire that their fidelity be permeated with humility and fervour, so that they may be true sons of the Church. They have no appetite either for sectarianism or ostentation. In their modest, scarcely tolerated position, they try to maintain what the Church has transmitted to them, confident that she has not revoked it, and strive to preserve the spirit of what they uphold.

It is obviously for the glory of God and the salvation of souls that tradition has transmitted to us the Latin and Gregorian rite of the holy Mass, the Breviary prior to the upheavals, the Roman Catechism, and the asceticism and discipline of the ecclesiastical and religious states. It is also for the love of God and the good of souls—beginning with our own—that we try to preserve these things, not driven by a spirit of contention or bitter zeal. In doing so, we have no doubt that we are sons of the Church. We do not in any way form a small marginal sect; we belong to the one Catholic, Apostolic, and Roman Church. To the best of our ability, we prepare for the blessed day when authority is restored, in full clarity, and the Church is at last delivered from the suffocating mists of the present trial. Although this day may be slow in coming, we try not to slacken in the essential duty of sanctifying ourselves. We do so by holding fast to tradition in the *same spirit of holiness in which we received it.*

We are no less members of the Church for picking and choosing among the Masses celebrated or the funeral rites being forced on families, often against the explicit wishes of the deceased. There is nothing schismatic about choosing between rites, prayers, and homilies, for the Church herself has taught us to exercise such discernment. I recall in this regard the anguished words of Louis Daménie, who was the director of *L'Ordre Français.* This was in late 1969, when the new Masses were taking over everywhere. "Until recently," he confided, "I went to Mass almost every day, picking whatever time best suited my schedule. I never worried about what kind of Mass I would find, no matter what church I walked into. But now I see so many variations and differences. I suffer so much from these casual, even sacrilegious communion rites, these debased rites contrary to the faith in the Real Presence, contrary to the function reserved to the priest. In short, so often do I run into Prot-estantized Masses everywhere, Masses that manifest neither faith nor piety, that I am obliged to abstain. *After all, the Church herself has taught me to do what I do: not to com-promise with what destroys the faith.* I have limited myself to a few chapels, but precisely because of this unavoidable limitation, I now rarely attend Mass during the week."

Who would dare claim that this exemplary Christian, making such a painful choice, stopped being a devoted son of the Church the moment he decided this? He made this choice precisely because he loved the Church as a son, knowing that our Mother the Church considers ambiguous rites abominable. A Church with an ambiguous liturgy would insult her Spouse, the Supreme Priest, and expose her faithful to mortal danger.

I hope our Catholic brothers who might think our choices arise from sectarian passion or attraction to schism will realize that we maintain traditional choices precisely to avoid breaking with Church discipline and losing our faith—to remain at the heart of Holy Church. Moreover, if our choices regarding the rites of the Mass, catechisms, burials, or baptisms opened a schismatic breach or proceeded from a diabolical root of rebellion, it would be proper that we be duly and formally condemned and judicially sanctioned. We are not. It is true that we are regarded with suspicion, viewed with ill will, ridiculed, or mocked, but this is far from legal condemnation.

It is because we belong to the Church, because we want to remain her docile and loving sons, that we have chosen not to go along with all these innovations, fully aware that their unspoken but certain aim is demolition, *self-demolition*. Moreover, it is abundantly clear that these innovations, multiplying without measure or restraint, are not being kept in check by ecclesiastical authorities.

Not only has the Church not excommunicated us for adhering to the doctrine and practice of the pre-Conciliar era, but all that we believe concerning the Church and her living stability persuades us that, without undue delay, and with complete clarity, she shall approve our attitude and consecrate it with her authority. We do not think, nor do we assert, that she will condemn all adaptation, bless sclerosis, or canonize stagnation. We merely say that, by virtue of her holy will to uphold true tradition, she will firmly reject ambiguous innovations that distort, weaken, and destroy tradition under the pretext of restoring its primitive purity or expanding its missionary reach.

As if, despite the frailty of churchmen, there existed any conflict between life and tradition, between tradition and zeal, or between tradition and life based on the Gospels. We hope in peace—not in slumber, but in vigilant fidelity—that the Church shall, without undue delay, raise her powerful voice and issue effective decrees making it clear that she shall not tolerate dubious catechisms, Protestantized Masses, the practical abolition of Latin in the liturgy, the practical suppression of the traditional Latin Roman Canon, nor the tendentious communion rite that subtly undermines faith in the Eucharist and in the priesthood. We refrain here from mentioning religious indiscipline and clerical anarchy, which constitute an outrage against the priesthood and an insult to the holy founders.

The day shall surely come when the Church, now briefly enduring what Jean Madiran so rightly calls an enemy occupation, shall very openly condemn all these so-called renewals that "modernistically" distort tradition. Along with these modernist novelties, she shall break the hidden powers who, from the depths of some Masonic lair, cunningly pull the strings and introduce into practice the Antichristian religion of evolving man. The day shall come when we shall sing, with the great classic that paraphrased Isaias:

> Jerusalem reborn more grand and beautiful!
> Whence on all sides repair to her
> The progeny not fostered in her bosom?
> Lift high, Jerusalem, lift high thy head!
> ...The people in thy light walk emulous.[5]

---

[5] Racine, *Athalie*, act 3, scene 7 (translated by J. Donkersley).

We are convinced that the post-Conciliar innovations are not of the Church, do not bind our obedience, and shall be manifestly rejected when the occupation of the Church comes to an end, because ultimately these upheavals, by their very nature, work to destroy the Church's fundamental mystery. Whether we see the Church as the temple and dwelling of God among men, or as the divinely assisted mediator of truth and grace; whether we regard her as the Body of Christ and His mystical extension—Jesus Christ poured forth and communicated—or as the spotless and unblemished Bride who dispenses supernatural goods to sinners, in intimate union with her Spouse and King—in any case, the ambiguous measures, the shifting ritual, the formless catechism, the morality without precepts, the religious discipline without obligation, the depersonalized hierarchical authority transferred to a fugitive and anonymous apparatus—none of these post-Conciliar inventions truly belong to the Church. We need not take them into account, since we are children of the Church and intend to remain so. We preserve tradition with patience. The occupying modernist forces will not be able to silence the sacred voice of our Mother for long. She will declare to us aloud that we cannot be better than to hold fast to tradition in holiness. *Patientia pauperum non peribit in finem*: the patience of the poor shall not be deceived forever.[6]

---

[6] Psalm 9:19.

APPENDIX 3

On the Church
and the Pope

"MY COUNTRY HAS HURT ME," wrote a young poet in 1944, in the midst of the purges, when the head of state we all know implacably pursued the sinister work planned for over four years.[1] "My country has hurt me." That is not the kind of truth one shouts from the rooftops. It is rather something one whispers to oneself, with deep sorrow, while still trying to hold onto hope. When I was in Spain, in the 1950s, I remember how carefully my friends, whatever their political leanings, avoided saying much about *la guerra nuestra*. Their country still hurt them. But what about when it is no longer a question of one's fatherland according to the flesh? What about when it is—certainly not about the Church herself, for she is absolutely unfailing and holy—but about the visible head of the Church? What about when it concerns the current holder of the Roman primacy?[2]

---

[1] Translators' note: The poet was Robert Brassilach, who under Charles de Gaulle was tried for collaboration with Germany during World War II and executed, despite the pleas of many leading French literary figures.

[2] Editor's note (1987): This was written in 1973.

How do we handle that, and what tone should we use when we quietly admit to ourselves: Ah! Rome has hurt me.

Of course the daily papers of the so-called "respectable" press will tell us that in two thousand years, Our Lord's Church has never seen such a splendid pontificate. But who takes these incorrigible maniacs of official flattery seriously? When we look at what is being taught and practised in the entire Church under today's pontificate, or rather, when we notice what has ceased being taught and practised; when we behold an ersatz Church that claims everywhere to be the real thing, yet no longer knows how to baptize children, bury the dead, celebrate the holy Mass worthily, or absolve sins in confession; when we witness the toxic tide of creeping Protestantization while the holder of supreme power refuses to give the energetic order to close the sluices; in short, when we are honest about what we see before us, we have no choice but to say: Ah! Rome has hurt me.

And we all know this is something quite different from those more or less private wrongs of which the holders of the Roman primacy have too often been guilty throughout history. In those cases, the victims, however badly they may have been harmed, could relatively easily extricate themselves by attending more diligently to their own sanctification. We must always attend to our sanctification. Yet what had never been seen before to this degree is that the wrong that the current occupant of Peter's chair allows consists in abandoning the very means of sanctification to the machinations of innovators and deniers. He permits the systematic undermining of sound doctrine, the sacraments, and the Mass. This casts us into unprecedented danger. While sanctification is certainly not rendered impossible, it is much more difficult. It is also much more urgent.

In such a perilous situation, is it still possible for the ordinary faithful, for the humble country or city priest, for the religious priest who finds himself increasingly a stranger in his own institute, for the religious sister who wonders whether she has been duped and deceived in the name of obedience — is it possible for all these little sheep of the immense flock of Jesus Christ and of His Vicar not to lose heart? Is it possible for them not to become the prey of a vast apparatus gradually forcing them to change their faith, their worship, their religious habit and religious life — in a word, to change their religion?

Ah! Rome has hurt me. One longs to repeat to one-self, with gentle precision, the words of truth, the simple words of supernatural doctrine learned in catechism, so that rather than adding to the evil, one might be deeply convinced by the teaching of revelation: that Rome shall one day be healed, and the ersatz Church will soon be unmasked by authority. At once it will crumble to dust, for its main strength comes from the fact that its intrinsic falsehood passes for truth, never having been effectively disavowed from above. One would wish, in the midst of so great a distress, to speak in words not too discordant with that mysterious discourse, wordless and silent, that the Holy Ghost murmurs in the heart of the Church.

But where to begin? Surely with the reminder of the fundamental truth concerning Jesus Christ's lordship over His Church. He willed a Church with the bishop of Rome at her head as His visible vicar as well as the bishop of bishops and of the entire flock. He granted upon him the prerogative of the rock so that the edifice would never collapse. He prayed that at least he among all the bishops would not shipwreck in the faith, so that, having recovered from the failings he shall not necessarily be spared, he might in the end confirm his brethren in the faith—or, if he himself does not do so, then one of his immediate successors.

Surely the first consoling thought that the Holy Ghost offers our hearts in these desolate days when Rome is partially invaded by darkness is that there is no Church without an infallible vicar of Christ endowed with primacy. Furthermore, no matter the failings, even in the religious sphere, of this visible and temporary vicar of Jesus Christ, it is Jesus Himself who governs His Church and His vicar in the government of the Church. He so governs His vicar that he cannot engage his supreme authority in upheavals or complicities that would change religion itself. So far extends, by virtue of the sovereignly efficacious Passion, the divine force of the rule of Christ ascended into heaven. He guides His Church both from within and from without, and He reigns over the hostile world. He makes His power felt to this perverse world, even and especially when the workers of iniquity, through modernism, not only penetrate the Church but also pass themselves off as the true Church.

Modernism works its mischief in two steps: first, it confounds parallel heretical authorities with the regular hierarchy whose strings they pull. Second, it exploits a supposedly universal pastoral reform that systematically conceals or distorts doctrinal truth and denies the sacraments or renders their rites uncertain. Modernism's cunning is to employ this infernal pastoral strategy both to corrupt the holy doctrine that God's Word entrusted to His hierarchical Church, and to alter or even nullify the sacred signs, bearers of grace, which the Church is faithfully to dispense.

There exists a head of the Church who is always infallible, always without sin, always holy, never failing or stopping in His work of sanctification. He alone is the true head, because all others, including the highest, hold authority only from Him and for Him. Now, *this holy and spotless head, completely set apart from sinners and raised above the heavens,* is not the pope, but He about whom the Epistle to the Hebrews speaks so magnificently: the Sovereign Priest, Jesus Christ.

Before mounting up to heaven and becoming invisible to our mortal eyes, Jesus, our Redeemer through the Cross, willed to establish for His Church, in addition to and above the numerous particular ministers, a single universal minister, a visible vicar who alone enjoys supreme jurisdiction. Jesus filled him with prerogatives: "Thou art Peter, and upon this rock I will build my church, and the gates of hell shall not prevail against it.... "[3] "Lord ... thou knowest that I love thee. Jesus saith to him: Feed my sheep ... feed my sheep...."[4] "I have prayed for thee, that thy faith fail not: and thou, being once converted, confirm thy brethren."[5]

Well then, if the pope is the visible vicar of Jesus Christ ascended to the invisible heavens, he is no more than a vicar: *vices gerens,* he stands in place, but remains distinct. Grace does not flow from the pope to give life to the mystical body. Grace flows solely from Our Lord Jesus Christ, for the pope just as much as for us. The same holds for the light of revelation. The pope holds a unique responsibility: guardianship over the means of grace, the seven sacraments as well as revealed truth. He receives unique assistance to serve as a faithful guardian and steward. But for this assistance to be effective, he must exercise his authority. Moreover, while he is protected from error when speaking infallibly, he can err in many other ways. Should he fail—in areas outside infallibility, of course—it

---

[3] Matthew 16:18–19.
[4] John 21:16–18.
[5] Luke 22:32.

does not prevent the Church's one true head, the invisible sovereign priest, from governing His Church. It would not affect the efficacy of His grace nor the truth of His law. It would not render him powerless to restrain the failings of his visible vicar. Nor would it prevent him from providing, without undue delay, a new and worthy pope to repair what his predecessor let spoil or destroy. A pope's shortcomings, weaknesses, and even partial betrayals never exceed his mortal lifetime.

Since ascending to heaven, Jesus has appointed two hundred sixty-three popes. Certainly, only a small number thereof proved themselves vicars so faithful that we invoke them as friends of God and holy intercessors. An even smaller number fell into very serious failings. The great majority of Christ's vicars have been reasonably adequate. None of them, while still pope, has committed or could commit treason to the point of explicitly teaching heresy with the fullness of his authority.

This being the situation of each pope and the succession of popes in relation to the head of the Church who reigns in heaven, we must not let a pope's weakness make us forget, even slightly, the solidity and holiness of Our Saviour's lordship. It must not blind us to the power and wisdom of Jesus, who holds even inadequate popes in His hand, confining their inadequacy within unbreachable bounds.

To have this confidence in the invisible and sovereign head of Holy Church, without denying that the visible vicar—the bishop of Rome, the keeper of the keys of the Kingdom of Heaven—is subject to real failings despite his prerogatives, we must place a realistic confidence in Jesus. This confidence does not evade the mystery of Peter's successor, with his heaven-guaranteed privileges as well as his human frailty. In order for any distress we feel because of the papacy to be absorbed by our theological hope in the

Sovereign Priest, our interior life must be oriented toward Jesus Christ, not the pope. Our interior life must embrace the pope and the hierarchy—this goes without saying—but it must be grounded not in them, but in the Divine Pontiff, in that priest who is the incarnate Redeemer, upon whom even the supreme visible vicar depends above all other priests.

Indeed, he is held in Jesus Christ's hand more than the others because he exercises a function with no parallel among the others.

Above all others, in a unique and supreme way, he cannot fail *to strengthen his brethren in the faith*; he himself or his successor.

The Church is not the pope's mystical body. The Church with the pope is Christ's mystical body. When Christians anchor their spiritual lives more and more in Jesus Christ, they do not despair even when they suffer agonies over a pope's failures, whether Honorius I, the competing popes at the end of the Middle Ages, or at the extreme, a pope who fails in the new ways modernism makes possible. When Jesus Christ is the heart and soul of Christians' interior lives, they do not need to lie to themselves about a pope's failures to retain confidence in his prerogatives. They know his failures will never go so far that Jesus would stop governing His Church because his vicar effectively prevented Him. A pope might well get close to the breaking point of changing Christianity itself through blindness, wishful thinking, or fatal delusion about a heresy like modernism. But even a pope who went that far could not strip away Our Lord Jesus' infallible rule, which still holds even a wayward pope in check and keeps him from ever using his heaven-given authority to actually pervert the faith.

An interior life properly anchored in Jesus Christ rather than in the pope cannot exclude the pope, without whom it would stop being a Christian interior life. An interior life properly anchored in the Lord Jesus therefore includes Christ's vicar and obedience to that vicar, but with *God served first*. This means such obedience, far from being unconditional, is always practiced in the light of theological faith and natural law.

We live by and for Jesus Christ, through His Church, which is governed by the pope, whom we obey in everything that falls within his proper authority. We do not live by and for the pope as if he had secured our *eternal redemption*, which is why Christian obedience cannot always, in every respect, equate the pope with Christ.

Usually, Christ's vicar governs in accordance with apostolic tradition well enough that obedient believers do not face major conflicts of conscience. But sometimes it can be otherwise. Although it is very exceptional, a believer might legitimately ask himself: how could I preserve tradition if I were to follow this pope's *directives*?

The interior life of a son of the Church who were to set aside the articles of faith regarding the pope, obedience to his legitimate orders, and prayer for him would cease to be Catholic. On the other hand, an interior life that includes pleasing the pope unconditionally—that is, blindly, in everything and always—is necessarily given over to human respect, is not free in regard to creatures, and exposes itself to all sorts of compromises and complicities. In his interior life, the true son of the Church, having wholeheartedly received the articles of faith relating to Christ's vicar, faithfully prays for him and willingly obeys him, but only in truth, that is, with apostolic tradition and, of course, natural law kept safe and intact.

It seems certain that too often a type of obedience toward the pope has been preached more concerned with effectiveness, with success in mass movements, than with

simple fidelity to the light, whatever the spectacular suc-
cesses might be. Not that concern for remaining within
apostolic tradition and fidelity to Jesus Christ was absent.
But what was most important, most active, most press-
ing was nevertheless to satisfy a man, to win his favour,
sometimes to advance one's career, to position oneself for
a cardinal's hat, or to gain prestige for one's order or congregation. But neither God nor service to the pope have
any need of our lies: *Deus non eget nostro mendacio*.

Let us recall the great prayer at the start of the
Roman Canon, a canon that Paul VI did not hesitate
to downgrade into general-purpose prayers adapted for
Calvinist-style suppers. (Reducing the Roman Canon in
this way has no basis in apostolic tradition and directly
opposes this unbreakable tradition.) In the Roman
Canon, after the priest has fervently asked the most
merciful Father through His Son Jesus Christ to sanctify the spotless sacrifice offered first *pro Ecclesia tua
sancta catholica*, the prayer continues: *una cum famulo
tuo Papa nostro . . . et Antistite nostro. . . .* The Church
has never intended to say *una cum* SANCTO *famulo tuo
Papa nostro et* SANCTO *Antistite nostro*, whereas she
does say *pro Ecclesia tua* SANCTA. Unlike the Church,
the pope is not necessarily holy. The Church is holy
even with sinful members—including ourselves—members who, alas, do not all strive toward holiness, or no
longer do so. It may well happen that the pope himself
belongs to this sorry category. God knows. In any case,
given the condition of the head of Holy Church—i.e.,
not necessarily that of a saint—we should not be scandalized if trials, even very harsh ones, befall the Church
on account of her visible head. We must not be scandalized that, as subjects of the pope, we cannot follow him
blindly or unconditionally in every matter.

The more our interior lives are anchored in the Church's invisible head—Our Lord Jesus, Sovereign Priest—the more they are nourished by apostolic tradition with its dogmas, Missal, and ritual, with that drive toward perfect love that is the heart of this holy tradition—the better we will handle having to become saints in a Church militant whose visible head, while protected from certain specific kinds of failure, remains nonetheless subject to the common condition of being a sinner.

Our Lord governs His Church through the pope and the hierarchy—the hierarchy subject to the pope—in such a way that the Church always remains secure in and fully conscious of her tradition, never ignorant or forgetful thereof. On the truths of the catechism, the celebration of the holy sacrifice and the sacraments, the basic hierarchical structure, the states of life, and the call to perfect love—in short, *on all the essential points of tradition*—the Church is assisted so that every baptized person with faith, whether bishop, pope, or layman, knows clearly where things stand.

Thus, an ordinary Christian, sticking to tradition on some major point known to all, refuses to follow a priest, bishop, episcopal conference, or even a pope would undermine tradition on that point, he is not showing, as some claim, displaying private judgement or pride. It is neither pride nor disobedience to recognize what tradition teaches on key points or to refuse to betray it.

For instance, whatever an episcopal conference or the secretary of a Roman congregation might scheme behind the scenes to make priests celebrate Mass without any outward sign of adoration or faith in the holy mysteries, every believer knows it is unacceptable to celebrate Mass while making this demonstration of unbelief. Someone who refuses to attend this Mass—or rather, such a ceremony that has usually ceased to be a Mass—is not exercising private judgement, nor is he a rebel. He is a believer rooted in the apostolic tradition, which no one in the Church can alter. For no one, regardless of rank—even the highest—has the authority to change the Church or her apostolic tradition.

I know that a priest who has not adopted the current pope's overhauled Missal and ritual but dares to declare, "I am with Rome! I uphold the apostolic tradition preserved by Rome," often gets treated as a fool or a fanatic. "You are with Rome?" some say, "Come now! How do you baptize? How do you celebrate Mass?" I answer: just as Paul VI himself did, up to 1970. In the centuries-old manner sanctioned by the popes before him. In the manner they, the bishops, and the priests of the Latin Church practised. I do what they all did when I keep the exorcisms at solemn baptism and when I offer the holy sacrifice according to an *Ordo Missæ* consecrated by fifteen centuries, never accepted by those who denied the holy sacrifice.

Moreover, if we the ministers of Jesus Christ who celebrate the Mass and the sacraments in this way, have broken with Rome or with the tradition Rome guarantees, why are we not punished with canonical sanctions *that only the vicar of Christ can lift?* I write this because it is true, and because I hope to reassure some faithful who cannot understand this glaring contradiction: being with Rome supposedly means adopting changes, in matters of faith or sacrament, that destroy apostolic tradition. No one can say, moreover, precisely how far the current Roman pontiff has claimed to exercise his authority in promulgating these changes. (Similarly, ten years after Vatican II, no one exactly knows the scope of that "pastoral" council's authority.) Once again, on all major points, apostolic tradition is perfectly clear. One need not examine it under a magnifying glass, nor be a cardinal or prefect of some

Roman dicastery, to recognize what contradicts it. It is enough to have been instructed in the catechism and liturgy before the modernist corruption.

All too often, in order to avoid breaking with Rome, the faithful and priests have been trained in a way that fosters a partly worldly fear, leaving them panicked, hesitant in their conscience, and unwilling to think critically the moment anyone accuses them of "not being with Rome." True Christian formation, by contrast, teaches us to be with Rome not through fear and blind obedience, but in clarity and peace, guided by a filial fear rooted in faith.

What do we care if our opponents mock us for supposedly being unable to tell the difference between what is merely contingent and changeable in tradition and what is essential and hence irreformable? Their mockery could affect us only if we were indeed foolish enough to treat everything claiming to belong to tradition equally. We do not.

We only say, and it is all that matters to us, that: first, on the major points, the Church's tradition is settled, certain, and irreformable; secondly, every Christian, however little instructed in his faith, knows these major points without hesitation; thirdly, that it is faith, not private interpretation, that lets us recognize them, just as it is obedience, piety, and love, not insubordination, that makes us uphold this tradition; fourthly, that any attempts by the hierarchy or papal weakness to overturn or allow the overthrow of this tradition shall one day be themselves overthrown, while the tradition shall triumph.

We are completely confident on this point: no matter what hypocritical weapons modernism places in the hands of episcopal conferences or even the vicar of Christ himself—hellish weapons that may mislead even their wielders—and however perfect these new weapons may be, the Church's traditions will prevail. The tradition of solemn baptism with its anathemas against the "accursed devil" will not long be set aside. The tradition of, in principle, absolving sins only after individual confession will not long be displaced. The tradition of the traditional Catholic Mass—Latin and Gregorian, with its language, Canon, and gestures faithful to the Roman Missal of Saint Pius V—shall soon be restored to honour. The tradition of the Catechism of Trent, or of a manual exactly like it, will flourish again soon.

On the major points of dogma, morality, the sacraments, states of life, and the perfection to which we are called, the Church's tradition is clear to all her members, regardless of rank. They hold fast to it with clear consciences, undeterred by the hierarchical guardians of this tradition, who try to intimidate, confuse, or even persecute them with the sophisticated cruelty of modernist executioners. They know, without a doubt, that by adhering to tradition they are not severing themselves from the visible vicar of Christ. For Christ rules over this visible vicar of Christ in such a way that he cannot alter or erase the Church's tradition, and even if he tries, he or his immediate successors will be obliged boldly to proclaim what lives eternally in the Church's memory: the apostolic tradition. The Bride of Christ shall not lose her memory.

To those who retort that tradition is synonymous with sclerosis, or that progress occurs by rejecting tradition—in short, to all those who are driven mad by the mirages of an absurd philosophy of becoming—I urge a careful reading of Saint Vincent of Lérins's *Commonitorium* and a close study of Church history: of her dogmas, sacraments, fundamental structures, and spiritual life. Thus they shall see the clear difference between "moving forward" and "going astray," between holding "advanced ideas" and "advancing according to right principles"; in short, between *profectus* and *permutatio*.

It is useful and salutary for us today more than in times of peace faithfully to meditate on the Church's trials. One might perhaps be tempted to see these trials merely as persecutions and attacks from without. Enemies from within, however, are much more to be feared: they know the weak spots better, they can strike or poison when least expected, and the scandals they provoke are much more difficult to overcome. For instance, in a parish, an anti-religious schoolteacher, no matter his efforts, will never corrupt the faithful as profoundly as a hedonistic and mod-ernist priest. Likewise, the defrocking of a simoniacal and traitorous cleric does not wreak such lasting harm.

In any case, it is certain a bishop who betrays the Cath-olic faith, even without being defrocked, inflicts upon the Church far more overwhelming a trial than some ordinary priest who takes a wife and ceases to offer the holy Mass. And beyond that, dare we even speak of a trial inflicted upon the Church of Jesus Christ by the pope himself, the vicar of Jesus Christ in person? This question alone makes many flinch and practically cry blasphemy. The mere thought tortures them. They refuse to face a trial of such gravity.

I understand their feelings. I know that a kind of ver-tigo can grip the soul when facing such enormities. *Sinite usque huc,*[6] Jesus said to the three apostles in His agony, as the high priest's soldiery came to seize Him, the sovereign and eternal priest, for judgement and death. *Sinite usque huc*: it is as if the Lord were saying: scandal can go even this far, but let it happen, and remember what I told you: "WATCH AND PRAY, FOR THE SPIRIT IS WILLING,

---

[6] Luke 22:51.

BUT THE FLESH IS WEAK."[7] *Sinite usque huc*: by consenting to drink the chalice, I have merited for you every
grace, even while you slept and left me utterly alone. I
have secured for you in particular a grace of supernatural
strength, mighty enough for any trial, even one that might
come to Holy Church through the pope's actions. I have
made it possible for you to escape even this vertigo.

Concerning this extraordinary trial, Church history
reveals what revelation about the Church does not. For
revelation about the Church nowhere states that the popes
shall never sin through negligence, cowardice, or worldli-
ness in the keeping and defense of the apostolic tradition.
We know that they shall never sin by leading men directly
to another religion; the nature of their office prevents that
sin. And when they exercise their authority at the level of
infallibility, it is Christ Himself who speaks and instructs
us, a privilege the popes receive from the moment they
become Peter's successors. But while Revelation assures
us of these papal prerogatives, nowhere does it state that,
when exercising his authority below the level of infallibility, a pope shall not play into Satan's hands and favour
heresy to some extent. Likewise, it is not written in Holy
Writ that, although he cannot formally teach another religion, a pope will never allow the sabotage of the conditions
necessary for defending the true religion. Modernism actually considerably favours such a defection.

Thus, Revelation concerning the pope nowhere guarantees that the vicar of Christ will never inflict upon the
Church the trial of certain grave scandals. I mean grave
scandals not merely in the sphere of private morality but
also in the properly religious sphere, and, so to speak, in
the ecclesial sphere of faith and morals. In fact, Church

---

[7] Matthew 26:41.

history shows us such trials from popes, although they have been rare and never enduring in their worst form. This should not be surprising, given how few canonized popes there have been since Saint Gregory VII. How few indeed the vicars of Christ who are invoked and venerated as friends and saints of God!

What is surprising is that popes who have endured terrible torments, such as Pius VI and Pius VII, have not been called saints either by the *Vox Ecclesiæ* nor the *Vox populi*. If *these* pontiffs, who suffered so much because they were popes, did not bear their trials with such love as to be canonized, why should we be surprised that other popes, who approach their office from a worldly angle, might commit serious failings or impose upon the Church formidable, heart-rending trials?

When faced with the extreme circumstance of having such popes, the faithful, priests, and bishops who wish to live by the Church take great care not only to pray for the Supreme Pontiff—then a source of great affliction for the Church—but they also cling ever more steadfastly to apostolic tradition: tradition concerning dogmas, the Mass, and the ritual; tradition on interior progress and the universal call to perfect love in Christ.

Here, the mission of Saint Dominic's son, Vincent Ferrer, is particularly illuminating. Among all the saints, this friar preacher is undoubtedly the one *who laboured most directly* for the papacy. Angel of judgement, legate *a latere Christi*, achieving the deposition of a pope after having shown him infinite patience, Vincent Ferrer was also, at the same time, an intrepid and kindly missionary, overflowing with wonders and miracles, proclaiming the Gospel to the vast throng of the Christian people. In his apostolic heart he carried not only the supreme pontiff—so enigmatic, stubborn, and harsh—but also Christ's entire flock, the multitude of the bewildered little people, the *turba magna ex omnibus tribubus et populis et linguis.*[8]

Vincent understood that the vicar of Christ's principal concern is not loyally serving Holy Church, far from it. The pope grants pride of place to satisfying his own obscure will to power. But if, at least among the faithful, the sense of life within the Church could be rekindled— the concern to live in accord with the dogmas and sacraments received from apostolic tradition—and if a pure and fervent wind of conversion and prayer were to sweep through this languishing and desolation Christendom, then, perhaps, there could finally come a vicar of Christ who is truly humble, with a Christian conscience about his supreme office and striving to fulfil it in the spirit of the Sovereign Priest.

Should the Christian people rediscover life in accordance with apostolic tradition, it shall become impossible for Jesus Christ's vicar to fall into grievous errors or to become complicit with falsehood in the defense and guardianship of this tradition. It would then become necessary for a good and perhaps saintly pope to succeed the bad or misguided pope without delay.

But, during these dark days when the Church's trial comes from the pope, too many faithful, priests, and bishops would like things to sort themselves out without them having to do anything or almost anything. At most they will agree to mutter a few prayers. They even falter at the thought of the daily Rosary: five decades each day offered to Our Lady in honour of Christ's hidden life, Passion, and glory. They show very little inclination, as far as they are concerned, to deepen their fidelity to apostolic tradition: dogmas, Missal, ritual, and interior life (for progress in the

---

[8] Apocalypse 7:9

interior life is evidently part of apostolic tradition). Having settled for lukewarmness in their own sphere, they are nevertheless scandalized that the pope, in his position as pope, is similarly lacking in fervour in preserving the apostolic tradition for the Church at large, that is, in faithfully fulfilling the unique mission entrusted to him. This way of seeing things is unjust. The more we need a holy pope, the more we must begin by setting our own lives, with God's grace and by holding to tradition, in the footsteps of the saints. Only then shall Our Lord Jesus grant to the flock the visible shepherd of which it has endeavoured to make itself worthy.

Let us not add our own particular negligence to the inadequacy or defection of the head. Let apostolic tradition at least be alive in the hearts of the faithful, even if for now it languishes in the heart and decisions of the one charged with responsibility over the Church. Then surely the Lord shall show us mercy.

For that to happen, our interior life must be referred not to the pope but to Jesus Christ. Our interior life, which obviously includes the truths of Revelation concerning the pope, must be oriented solely toward the Sovereign Priest, Our Lord and Saviour Jesus Christ, in order to overcome the scandals that come to the Church through the pope.

That is Saint Vincent Ferrer's timeless lesson during these apocalyptic times when we are witnessing one of the major failings of the Roman pontiff. But with modernism we are experiencing even more terrible trials. All the more reason for us to live more purely, in all respects, according to apostolic tradition. In all respects, including that crucial point about which scarcely anyone speaks since the death of the Dominican Father Réginald Garrigou-Lagrange: the *effective* tendency towards the perfection of charity. And yet the moral doctrine revealed by Our Lord and transmitted by the apostles states that we must tend towards perfect love, since the law of growth in Christ is proper to the grace and charity which unite us to Christ.

The dogma concerning the pope is both transcendent and obscure: the pontiff is the universal vicar of Jesus Christ but is nevertheless not exempt from failings, even grave ones, which may be very dangerous for his subjects. Yet the dogma of the Roman pontiff is but one aspect of the more fundamental mystery of the Church. Two great propositions introduce us into this mystery:[9] first, the Church, although recruited from among sinners like us, remains the infallible dispenser of light and grace, dispensing them by means of a hierarchical organization governed from heaven by her head and Saviour Jesus Christ and assisted by His Spirit. Further, here on earth the Saviour offers the perfect sacrifice through His Church and nourishes Her with His very substance. Secondly, the Church, being Our Lord Jesus' holy Bride, must share His Cross, including the Cross of betrayal by her own members. Yet she never ceases to be sufficiently assisted in her hierarchical structure, beginning with the pope, and to burn sufficiently with charity. In short, she remains at all times sufficiently pure and holy to share in the trials of her Bridegroom, even the betrayal of certain hierarchs, while preserving intact her inward mastery and supernatural strength. Never shall the Church succumb to vertigo.

If, in our interior life, we rightly place the Christian truth concerning the pope within the wider Christian truth concerning the Church, we shall overcome in truth the scandal of all falsehoods, including those that may befall the Church through the Vicar of Christ or through the successors of the apostles. In this respect, at least with

---

[9] See our book *Mystères du Royaume de la Grâce*, vol. 1, ch. 7.

regard to the bishops, Saint Joan of Arc is an incomparable model. For our part, within the limits of our poverty, we shall strive to be faithful to what was one of Saint Joan of Arc's particular graces.

When we think about the current pope,[10] the modernism that has taken hold, apostolic tradition, and perseverance in that tradition, we find ourselves increasingly reduced to consider these questions only through prayer, an urgent supplication for the whole Church and for him who today holds the keys to the Kingdom of Heaven. He holds them in his hands yet, so to speak, does not use them. He leaves the gates of the sheepfold open to the path trodden by brigands. He fails to close those protective gates that his predecessors had invariably kept shut with unbreakable locks and secure bolts. Sometimes he even pretends to open what must forever remain closed; such is the confusion of post-Vatican II ecumenism.

We are necessarily reduced to thinking of the Church only by praying for her and for the pope. This is actually a blessing. Yet to think of our Mother, the Bride of Christ, in so pitiful a state does not lessen our determination to see things clearly. May this essential clarity, without which all our strength would fade, be so steeped in humility and gentleness that we might move the High Priest to hasten to our aid. *Deus in adjutorium meum intende, Domine ad adjuvandum me festina.* May it please Him to entrust us to his most holy Mother, Mary Immaculate, to bring us the remedy we need as soon as possible.

---

[10] Editor's note (1987): This was written in 1973.

The Fog of "Revelationism" and the Light of Faith

I CALL "REVELATIONISM" A *DISOR-dered* trust in private revelations, one that is not sufficiently corrected by reason and by faith. To be clear, I do not reproach these brethren in the faith for believing in miracles of a private order, nor in its indispensable role within the Church. Rather, I take issue with their placing them in practice above Scripture and Tradition, with their treating the most diverse miraculous events as if they were equivalent; and finally with allowing their interior life to be thrown off course by the miraculous, instead of subjecting it to the rule of the theological virtues, which are the true centre of all life in Christ.

We thus find certain Christians who give childish and bizarre revelations, supposedly received by privileged souls, exactly the same credit as the clear, sober, and doctrinally sound messages of Lourdes. Worse still, others lean on visions of those privileged souls to claim to know far more about Our Lord's Passion than the evangelists themselves.

Since these revelationists talk so much about the Lord's judgements upon the course of human history, let us remember the lessons of Revelation as the inspired Scriptures convey them.[1] Let us also recall, on the same subject, the solid teaching of the Fathers and doctors. We believe in the return of Our Lord: *Credo . . . in unum Dominum Jesum Christum . . . et iterum venturus est cum gloria judicare vivos et mortuos, cujus regni non erit finis.*

Not only at the very end shall the faith be nigh extinguished and charity survive only in a few, so deeply shall coldness and selfishness have sown death in souls, but even before that, history shall show early signs of this darkening and fading of spiritual life. Christians have always known, especially since the Apostle Saint John and since Saint Augustine, that a final Antichrist would come, but that he has had precursors from apostolic times.[2]

The book of the Apocalypse, to which one rightly refers in order to speak properly about the end of the world, cannot be considered as a timeline laid out in advance. It is a theology of history expressed in symbols that repeat themselves with growing clarity.[3] Another key reference is Matthew 24, along with the latter part of Luke 17 and 21. These fundamental texts must be interpreted carefully, for they do not speak solely and exclusively of two generations, the generation that saw Christ's first coming and the temple's destruction and the final one that shall see Jesus Christ's glorious return. These chapters also address, in many ways, the generations in between. Our Lord has judged worthy of His infallible teaching on the judgements He enacts on the course of history the numerous intermediate generations which would include by far the largest number of the faithful and make up the most important portion of His Church.

---

[1] See the chapters on Jesus the Sovereign Judge in our book *Les Grandeurs de Jésus-Christ.*

[2] 1 John 2:18.

[3] The classic work on this issue is *L'Apocalypse* by Father Allo, O. P.

One sign of the end will have no prior precedent: the conversion of the Jews as a people. But no one can say exactly when even this sign will take place before the world's end. In the case of the other signs—apostasy, the Antichrist, the spread of the Gospel, spiritual death, wars, and cataclysms—we know that they shall not only unfold in *a sort of linear progression*, but that they also advance in *something like cyclical repetitions*. Which of these cycles we are living through now, God only knows.

God has given a double revelation to the intermediate generations between the one that witnessed the destruction of Jerusalem and the one that shall see the end of the world. Even as He announces the overflowing of iniquity and terrible retributions, He assures us that the wellsprings of courage and consolation shall endure. However much iniquity waxes in the course of history, these perilous times of trial shall be shortened for the sake of the elect.[4] Moreover, no one shall be able to snatch the sheep from the Good Shepherd's hands.[5] Thirdly, Redemption shall not cease to be nigh, and we shall have to lift our heads— *levate capita vestra*[6]—towards Him whose Heart is open to us.[7] Fourthly, the Holy Ghost shall not cease bearing witness to Christ,[8] even when apostasy shall seem to have submerged everything. In sum, "the gates of hell shall not prevail against" the Church,[9] against Peter, against the faith, against the Mass,[10] or against the sacraments,

---

[4] Matthew 24:22.
[5] John 10:28–29.
[6] Luke 21:28.
[7] John 19:37.
[8] John 16:1–15.
[9] Matthew 16:18.
[10] On this very subject, the permanence of the Mass, see Thomas Malvenda, O. P., *Dissertation sur l'Antichrist*, n. 22, which follows 2 Thessalonians in the *Bible de Vence*, vol. 16 (Paris, 1773). This Bible takes up and completes the *Bible de Dom Calmet*.

even when the "man of sin" shall sit in the holy place.[11]

There is therefore a double revelation concerning divine judgements and punishments. The contrasting aspects must not be isolated and separated. Private revelations concerning interventions of divine justice must faithfully align with this perspective of canonical revelation. Comminatory prophecies are an integral part of the Gospel of Jesus Christ. Our merciful Saviour presents Himself as king and as judge, not merely as judge at world's end but in the course of history. *Ipsius sunt tempora et sæcula.*[12] The prophecies of Jerusalem's destruction, the terrible end of the world, and the persecutions of Christians are inseparable from the Gospels and Epistles. On several occasions, Jesus spoke as a *prophet of calamity. But He is a prophet of calamity* within a Gospel atmosphere, and this changes everything, making His prophecy nourishment for living through divine grace, a source of inner peace and beatitude. *Beati qui lugent quoniam ipsi consolabuntur.*[13]

Thus, we must not dismiss private prophecies just because they are prophecies of calamity; indeed, we should take them seriously precisely for that reason. But we require two things: first, sufficient evidence to confirm that the messenger or visionary speaks on God's behalf and *in His name*, rather than from personal invention. This presupposes a second condition: that their prophecy aligns with the Gospel's spirit of peace, conversion, and supernatural balance. In short, private prophecies, even comminatory ones, must reflect the elevation, sobriety, and purity characteristic of the Gospel.

We now offer some more immediately practical guidelines for how we should act in the present time. At this moment, when the celebration of Mass is gravely

---

[11] 2 Thessalonians 2:4 and Matthew 24:15
[12] Blessing of the Paschal candle at the Easter Vigil.
[13] See *Summa Theologiae*, IIa-IIae, q. 174, a. 1, ad 2.

threatened, we need to uphold it all the more, that is, to say and attend it *with the requisite dispositions*. At this moment, when the true catechism is hard to come by, we need to dedicate ourselves to it all the more. At this moment, when family laws (if they can be called that) are criminal and monstrous, we must fight them tooth and nail. At this moment, when Paul VI's innovations are rightly met with suspicion, as the devastating evidence in the Abbé of Nantes's *Libellus* makes clear, we need to have courage to recognize that we are not bound by *this* pontiff's novelties.[14] At this moment, when bishops, kneaded and manipulated by collegiality, try to impose a religious syncretism that is at once Masonic, communist, and Christian, let us recognize that we are not bound to follow them. And finally, at this moment we must bear witness to the faith of the ages with a strength and humility that must be renewed without ceasing, for we are not facing a violent persecution, which would make things a lot simpler, but a modernist revolution inspired by the demons of the worst kind of confusion.

Such is the present moment. Such is our diagnosis, informed by the reason God has given us and enlightened by the lights of faith and theological reflection. It is therefore at this moment, such as it is, that we must sanctify ourselves and bear witness, and this all the more as we ask God that, in the years to come, Saint Pius X's prophecy may be fulfilled in some way. More than ever, the present moment demands from Christians a spiritual attitude of lucidity, realism, faith, charity, and hope. But these reasonable and theological attitudes are exactly what the producers and peddlers of revelationist writings fail to encourage in well-meaning souls.

---

[14] Editor's note (1987): This was written in 1973. See our articles "Ce principe très simple" in *Itinéraires* 168 (December 1972) and "L'Église dispensatrice des sacrements" in *Itinéraires* 171 (March 1973).

When it comes to private prophecy within the Church, some seem to focus on a single aspect: the announcement of divine chastisements. *Yet there are other aspects*, not opposed to the first, certainly, but of a higher order, namely, doctrinal charisms, such as the teaching of wisdom, the *sermo sapientiæ* granted to certain great saints for the edification of souls. This *sermo sapientiæ* is not, strictly speaking, a charism granted to women,[15] although one must acknowledge that a message such as the "little way" taught by Saint Thérèse bears the mark of a true charism. It is to unduly narrow the favours bestowed by the Spirit of Christ upon the Church to see charisms only in the admonitory messages given in apparitions, even when those messages are orthodox and the visionary worthy of belief.

One of the revelationists' most serious failings is that they have not seriously meditated on the life and death of the saints, men and women, who were most deeply engaged in private prophecy, apparitions, the marvellous, and the miraculous, such as Joan of Arc, Margaret Mary Alacoque, Catherine Labouré, Bernadette Subirous, and the children of Fatima. The lives and deaths of these privileged authentic visionaries were marked by simplicity, calm, and clarity, free from panic or exaltation. Their messages were as straightforward as can be, devoid of complexity. For them they were ready to give their lives, and indeed Saint Joan of Arc was a martyr. Yet Joan and the others did not anchor their souls in some *isolated or exaggerated* realm of the marvellous. Like all Christians and all saints, they grounded them in faith, hope, and charity. They held to their message only because it formed part of the exceptional duty

---

[15] On this subject, see *Summa Theologiae*, IIa-IIae, q. 177, the treatise on states of life, as it is called. The end of IIa-IIae actually contains *three* major treatises. The one on the states of perfection comes last, after the treatises on charisms (graces *gratis datæ*) and forms of life (active or contemplative).

that God commanded them to fulfil, just as He commands ordinary duties to most, *ordinary* duties that we must fulfil with *perfect* love. They held to their message only because that primary fidelity was for them the condition of living the theological virtues and the gifts of the Holy Ghost. There the soul of their spiritual life lay. Their existence cannot be imagined apart from the marvellous, nor apart from their fidelity in bearing witness to it. Yet the heart of their life was not the marvellous, but charity.

The marvellous revelations and prophecies of which they were faithful messengers are indispensable to the existence and holiness of the Church, as well as to the conversion and survival of France. The mystical body cannot do without graces *gratis datæ* here on earth. But it is grace *gratum faciens*, the grace of the virtues and gifts, that is its living soul. Joan, Margaret Mary, Catherine Labouré, Bernadette, and the children of Fatima were messengers of the most extraordinary marvels, and while communicating and defending their message they never stopped growing stronger in sanctifying grace in a love at once humble and firmly grounded in reality. Hence their message, not only because of the balance of its content but by the manner of its transmission, brought not alarm but peace, both for them and for their neighbour.

The Church does not and cannot reject marvels, revelations, or miracles. But she places the theological life and holiness far above these, beyond all comparison. Remaining faithful to this principle, we neither dismiss the marvellous out of hand nor embrace it with foolish credulity or anxious agitation. Rather, giving those private revelations that deserve trust (especially those of universal significance) their proper place, we should make the best use of them in the light of faith, that "faith that worketh by charity."[16]

---

[16] Galatians 5:6.

For the Christian to live rightly within the Church, it is not enough for him to say: the teaching of the hierarchical Magisterium suffices; if there is anything else, I do not wish to know it. For the Magisterium itself is obliged to know that there is something else, certainly not a teaching different from the one the hierarchy holds and safeguards, but other miraculous voices of faithful messengers who have a mission to speak in order to draw attention to that very teaching which the Magisterium dispenses. There is no Magisterium other than that of the hierarchy, no higher inspired Magisterium superior before which the hierarchy should lower its flag. But there are other messengers than those of the hierarchy. There are inspired and miraculous messengers whom the hierarchical dignitaries must deign to hear, though it remains for the hierarchy alone to give judgement and decision. The Catholic notion of the Church does not exclude charisms, but it subordinates them to the hierarchy. It does not dismiss private revelations, but does require that they not be illusions and that they align fully with Revelation.

Throughout the Church's history, the true hierarchy— not the insinuations of the modernist hierarchy—had never tried to silence inspired and miraculous voices. The true hierarchy, which, in an ordinary and official manner, is endowed with the *charism of truth* (Saint Irenaeus), knows that these voices, if they come from God, do not contradict Revelation, but repeat it and make it understood. They reach hearts with a more penetrating tone, one better suited to new situations, as it were. Thus the words of the hierarchical Magisterium concerning the Sacred Heart of Jesus were not altered by Saint Margaret Mary's private revelations. Rather, after those revelations the same words were spoken with greater vehemence and echoed with greater fervour. In 1854, the Roman Pontiff's

mighty voice resounded in the infallible definition of the
Immaculate Conception, but only after the apparitions of
the Immaculate to Saint Bernadette did this voice set the
multitudes in motion and rally the nations to prayer and
penance. The same could be said concerning devotion to
the Rosary and consecration to the Immaculate Heart of
Mary: without the inspired voice of the seers of Fatima,
the voice of the ordinary Magisterium would never have
struck so deeply into Christian souls. And what about
admonitory private revelations? The warnings of Matthew
24 are still there, and the Church always proclaims them
on the last Sunday after Pentecost; only the modernist
liturgy tries to make men forget them. The Church keeps
sounding the oracles of Matthew 24 to ears of the faithful, but in order that these warnings be taken seriously by
modern Christians—wandering in sin, dulled in spirit, as
the men of Noah's day on the very eve of the flood—in
order to awaken the sleepers, the teaching of the hierarchical Magisterium on divine judgments must not be modified
or twisted in a millenarian direction, but faithfully echoed
in the course of history by messengers charged with trans-
mitting admonitory revelations. All that is asked of these
messengers is that they present adequate credentials and
that their message is in harmony with the Gospel.

All this to say that private revelations, and indeed
all charisms, have their rightful place in the life of the
Church. Their role is not incidental, still less superfluous, but necessary. Yet they must be rightly ordered:
subordinated to the authority of the true Magisterium
(as opposed to the counterfeit modernist Magisterium),
situated firmly within the line of divine Revelation, and
allowing us to be awakened, moved, converted, and edi-
fied by the miraculous tone in which they repeat to us the
words of eternal life.

A Doctrinal Note on the
Mystery of Christ the King

UST LIKE THE MYSTERIES OF
Christ the Saviour and Christ the Sovereign Priest,
the mystery of Christ the King is a revealed truth.
To study it profitably, one must begin with Revelation as
found in Scripture and as expounded by the Magisterium,
especially in the encyclical *Quas Primas*. Reflecting in harmony with the analogy of faith, we shall come to understand the distinctive character of Christ's kingship and the
way in which it extends to the human race.

Our reflection risks shipwreck on a double reef:
either we understand the essence of Jesus Christ's kingship —converting souls and uniting them to their Saviour—
but neglect the extension of this kingship—building a civilization of a spirit and form that accords with historical
circumstances; or, contrariwise, having grasped that men
are not angels and that the structures of the city greatly
assist either their perdition or their conversion, we understand the *extension* of Jesus Christ's reign to the values of
civilization, but lose sight, at least partially, of the *essential* nature of this kingship, seeing only its social dimension. Some rightly situate Christ's kingdom in the order

of charity but fail to see that it must unavoidably spread its benefits to minds and bodies. Others see clearly that Christ's kingdom must influence minds and bodies, but they do not understand that this influence is derivative, an overflow of the former. For the social aspect of the kingship of Christ, although real and incontestable, remains derivative. Yet this extension is not artificial; it belongs to the nature of things. Because he is an interior king—king in the secret of souls, king of conversion—Jesus Christ must be king in the domestic, professional, economic, political orders.

Let us say at the outset that the domestic, professional, economic, and political orders are governed by their own laws that are not identical to those of the interior life and conversion of heart. Christ's reign in these different areas, therefore, demands not only that Christians live religiously but that they acknowledge the proper laws governing these areas. Indeed, religious life would not deserve the name if it disregarded these proper laws or treated them as irrelevant.

In reading Scripture, both the Old Testament and the Gospel, one cannot fail to notice the difference between how God's kingdom is fulfilled in the Gospel and how it was foretold in the Psalms and prophets. The inspired seers had indicated that God would reign through holiness and purity of heart, and even through humiliations and the Cross. The Christian liturgy's *regnavit a ligno Deus* aptly summarizes one of the aspects of the ancient prophecy. But only one. There was another prominent perspective held that God's reign would bring about a dazzling and radical political transformation. This was what many Israelites expected, and it was at least partially in harmony with the "oracles of Yahweh." Nevertheless, Jesus Christ always refused to satisfy this vehement aspiration that often made far too much noise. Each time the disciples wanted to make him king and get him to play a role on the strictly political arena, he slipped away. He had already answered Satan, who offered him the earth and its kingdoms at the beginning of his public ministry: *Vade retro Satana*—get behind me, Satan.

Reflecting on the unexpected and often disconcerting way in which Israel's inspired prophecies were accomplished, and reflecting upon the discrepancy between figure and reality, Father Marie-Joseph Lagrange wrote these luminous words:

> When Jesus Christ appeared, the question arose, as Pascal grasped, of whether God cared more about the worldly glory of the Jews than the salvation of souls, more about the temporal welfare of one nation than the moral reform of all peoples, more about the triumph of Jewish arms than the victory each man would win through grace over passions and sin. When the apostles recognized in Jesus of Nazareth the one sent to earth by God to teach mankind to love God and neighbour—which was the whole Law—and to be perfect as their heavenly Father is perfect, and to reconcile them to God through His Blood and death; when, seeing that He had risen and ascended to heaven, they recognized that He was truly the Son of God, they judged that before this supreme, unexpected, and ineffable gift of God all Israel's dreams paled as mere carnal hopes, narrow and unworthy of God. Having lived with the Son of God, they deemed that even a glorious king would cut a poor figure beside Him.
>
> The immense outpouring of grace whereof they were instruments appeared to them as a divine work that rendered Israel's territorial ambitions superfluous. Could one fault God for not fulfilling His promise to His people when He entrusted them with calling all nations to true

salvation? To grasp this ... it sufficed to have a religious soul, a desire that God be known and loved, and to value His glory above Israel's. This is precisely what Pascal means, and we must listen to him: "In these promises each one finds what he has most at heart, temporal benefits or spiritual, God or the creatures; but with this difference, that those who therein seek the creatures find them, but with many contradictions, with a prohibition against loving them, with the command to worship God only, and to love Him only, which is the same thing, and, finally, that the Messias came not for them; whereas those who therein seek God find Him, without any contradiction, with the command to love Him only, and that the Messias came in the time foretold, to give them the blessings which they ask."[1]

That Jesus Christ is the Sovereign Priest poses no difficulty for us. We know that Jesus Christ's coming had a religious aspect, that of prayer, forgiveness of sins, and the rites that draw us closer to God. We can see that the title of priest suits him fully when, for example, we hear his answer to the Samaritan woman: "The hour cometh, and now is, when the true adorers shall adore the Father in spirit and in truth";[2] when we see Him forgive the sins of Mary Magdalene or of the paralytic; and when he gave to the apostles the power to forgive sins in turn. When we read that He established the rite of the new covenant in His blood, poured out in the chalice for the multitude of men, we cannot doubt that He holds and exercises a properly priestly power. It may have been otherwise for the Jews addressed in the Epistle to the Hebrews, for

---

[1] *Pensées*, 674 in Brunschvicg's numbering, trans. Trotter, 176. Father Marie-Joseph Lagrange, O. P., "Pascal et les prophéties messianiques," in *Revue Biblique* (October 1906): 550.

[2] John 4:24.

whom His priesthood might have been a matter of doubt or difficulty because of its profound and fundamental differences with the Levitical priesthood. For us, after twenty centuries of Christian faith and after the destruction of the Temple of Jerusalem and the cessation of worship there, the question of the Levitical priesthood is only of historical interest and in no way prevents us from grasping the validity of this point of our belief: Christ is truly a priest; He is the Sovereign Priest.

On the other hand, belief in Christ the King can be harder to understand, precisely because the title "king" does not refer primarily to something religious. While "priest" is a term rooted in religion, bringing to mind prayer, rites, and a religious community, "king" belongs to the political sphere, suggesting political communities, harmony, and a good and honest social organization. Yet, as any Christian must acknowledge, Jesus Christ came in a religious capacity. His person and mission are oriented toward the spiritual rather than the political. How then should we understand His title of king? Especially when we recall that He Himself claimed this title before Pilate, and that the Catholic Church, His perfectly intelligent and inspired Spouse, has established a feast to honour his royal dignity.

As difficult as it may seem, we must avoid conceiving Our Lord's kingship in political terms. Scripture does not support it, and doing so would do violence to the common tradition of Christianity. We must resolutely deny that Jesus Christ is a political king, and that He exercises power like the governments of this world. I am well aware people talk a great deal about the social kingship of Our Lord, and rightly so, as we shall see. We shall also see that this lordship over civil society, real as it is, cannot be compared to the lordship of any king, emperor, governor, or dictator. It is something different from the lordship of the great men of this world. It is of a spiritual nature, even if its effects on temporal matters are necessary and inevitable. You may think that in rejecting a political conception of Our Lord's kingship I am playing into the hands of secularism and the secularization of civil institutions. Have a little patience; you shall see that this is not so. You shall see that, far from endorsing secularism, affirming the unique, spiritual nature of Christ's reign directly refutes it.

The more we seek to counter the ideas of those who, like the faithless Jews, insist, "We will not have this man reign over us,"[3] the more we must strive to guide those who have gone astray, and the more we need to present to them the true nature of Jesus Christ's reign. His is an interior reign; it belongs to the religious sphere. You might ask: "You have already told us that Jesus Christ is priest in the religious sphere. Is that not enough? Why must we also call Him king?" In truth, the surpassing excellence of the Son of God, Saviour of men, requires multiple terms to convey it. The title of king does not overlap with that of priest, but adds to it, namely that just as an earthly king rules a political community according to law, so Jesus Christ governs the multitude of men in a government of sanctification through a law of grace and the Holy Ghost. This government cannot remain disconnected from earthly societies. In short, calling Our Lord "king" complements the title "priest," adding the ideas of universality, the law of grace, and His influence upon civil society.

We must turn to the crucial text: Jesus' response to Pontius Pilate. It leaves no doubt about the interior nature of the kingdom he came to establish. Already His refusal to let the crowd of the Jews proclaim Him king after the miracle of the multiplication of loaves, and even more

---

[3] Luke 19:14.

clearly his rebuke to Satan who offered Him the kingdoms of the earth, put the kingdom he came to establish in true perspective. But the dialogue with the Roman governor, at the very moment of His death sentence, is even clearer and more explicit: "My kingdom is not of this world. If my kingdom were of this world, my servants would strive that I should not be delivered to the Jews: but now my kingdom is not from hence. Pilate therefore said to him: Art thou a king then? Jesus answered: Thou sayest that I am a king. For this I was born, and for this came I into the world: that I should give testimony to the truth. Every one that is of the truth heareth my voice."[4] These words evidently mean that Jesus' kingdom is not akin to any of the others. It does not defend itself with their same means. And, especially, it is not at the same level. It is at the intimate heart of man, at the depths where man hears the truth coming from on high, the word of life that delivers, converts, and saves him.

The kingdom of Jesus Christ is interior, spiritual, and located in the secret of the heart, in the sanctuary when man hears the voice of grace. Therefore, His kingdom is ecclesial: it is realized in both the intimacy of our souls and within the whole Church. This can be easily understood. In the Church, interiority and society are not opposed, but coincide. The Church is the only society located at the level of the heart's secret, that ultimate recess where the soul communicates with God. For the words the Church speaks are the very words of God, and the sentiments that develop within the Church are those of grace and divine love.

Well then! Christ's reign is inseparably interior and ecclesial. Even if some Christians' scandalous behaviour should revolt us and lead us into temptation, we must

---

[4] John 18:36–37

not create a false dichotomy between personal interior life and life in the Church. The teaching of the Gospel alone should suffice. As we have already emphasized, the kingdom Jesus came to establish is religious, a religion of conversion and communion with God, proclaimed or intimated throughout the Gospel. Yet, however hidden or mystical this reign may be, Jesus never suggested that it could exist without rites or ministers, or outside the Church. The interior religion He founded is intrinsically ecclesial. Strip from the Gospel (and from Saint Paul) all references to the Eucharist, the priesthood, preaching guided by the Holy Spirit, and the hierarchy that must endure; remove the passages connecting the living Bread with the theological life, and union with God with the Church's divine powers; in short, try to keep from the Gospel only what is interior while rejecting what is visible and juridical, and you strip away even what is interior. Such a Gospel is no longer genuine. In Scripture as it is written and as we read it, Jesus Christ's reign is both interior and tied to a society with hierarchical authority, and interior precisely because it pertains to this supernatural society and its divine powers.

Furthermore, Christian sensibility has no hesitation on this point. A Christian who longs for gentleness, humility, purity, and selfless service to others, who seeks to be wholly devoted to God and to the salvation of his brethren, and who aspires to holiness and the imitation of Christ, shall never neglect the Eucharist or disregard the teachings imparted by the priestly hierarchy. Priests may disappoint; as in Saint Paul's time, the ministers of the Gospel can mix their own passions and interests with the sacred message[5] so much that discerning it requires childlike simplicity and heroic generosity. Nevertheless the Christian disciple of

---

[5] 1 Philippians 1:17.

Jesus Christ who aspires to the *sanctification of His name and the coming of His reign* shall never think of separating himself from the Church. The more he experiences that the Church is not to be confused with the weakness or malice of some of her members, the more he will strive to live fully within her and contribute, both inwardly and outwardly, to her growth in merit and number.[6] Thus, it is clear that Christ's reign is interior, *within* a supernatural hierarchical society and *through* that society.

"All this is very fine and even true," some father or mother might say, "but meanwhile, the laws and customs of my country make the task of educating children — already difficult enough in itself — extremely hard. Divorce is spreading, corrupt films proliferate, and the school system tends toward State monopoly. Together these things create a crushing social pressure that does little to foster the reign of Jesus Christ in the souls of the young. I understand that, whatever the circumstances, and even in the best of situations, children (and adults too) will sooner or later be tempted to think and act badly, whether through the fault of the wicked or that of those who call themselves good. But it is one thing to be led astray through some individual encounter; it is quite another to be scandalized by the whole fabric of social life. Scandal receives from customs and laws a virulence, scope, and credibility that no single man could give it. When it is enshrined in law, propagated as an idea, and expressed through art, it increases its power tremendously. You rightly remind us that Jesus Christ did not will political rule and that He refused Caesar's power." Should a father then conclude that he should form his children for spiritual life without worrying about a society that scandalizes them? The

---

[6] *Ut populus Christianus et numero et merito augeatur* (several orations in the Missal).

answer must be no. Since men are not disembodied spirits, the salvation of souls requires that the kingship of Jesus Christ extend over society.

The case of the father or mother I just proposed is immediately clear, even to someone with no political experience. But plenty of other examples are just as easy to understand. Consider the situation in France regarding medicine, industry, or the representation of intermediate bodies. Medicine is on the verge of becoming no more than a former liberal profession, and doctors risk becoming civil servants. In many businesses, the state is becoming the main stakeholder and taking over from citizens in the task of management. The representation of intermediate organizations is very poorly ensured. These are all clear signs of how the state is taking over everywhere, muscling in on areas that are not its business. It is a kind of tyranny that might be relatively gentle and hidden, but real nonetheless. Should we say that these are certainly regrettable abuses, but have nothing to do with Christ's kingship, or have only the most tenuous connection with it? If we have a sense of the interiority of religion, we would be inclined to think so. But if our sense of interior religion becomes sharper and purer, we will change our perspective. Anyone who wants Jesus Christ to reign in his own heart and those of his brethren will not be satisfied knowing his brethren are being scandalized by their environment, that society's very structure is corrupting their hearts. He will fiercely reject a scandalous society. And a statist society is a scandalous society. It reduces man to a mere subject with ever less responsibility. It makes of him nothing more than a cog in a machine. In such a society, virtue, honour, uprightness, and generosity do not thrive—on the contrary, they wither.

Holy Church, which is the kingdom of God among men, has therefore not ceased to denounce statism for a century now. She carries on the struggle for a political order that is not scandalous but in conformity with natural law for the sake of the eternal salvation of her children. She does so also for the sake of the peace and welfare of civil society. Yet the main reason for her interventions, teachings, and exhortations, is indeed the eternal salvation of souls and the mystical reign of her Spouse. One need only read and listen.

Hence, in explaining the mystery of Christ the King, I can be sure I do not miss the mark if I go beyond the mystical revelations of Scripture to seek out the basic principles of natural law, and if I touch upon such matters as the standing of the liberal professions, industry, or the representation of citizens.

Likewise, a century ago, the dockworkers of Marseilles did not imagine that to live as Christians it was enough simply to hear Mass on the feast of the guild's patron saints. Their faith in the Lord and their desire to serve Him moved them to frame, "under the glorious patronage of Saints Peter and Paul and Our Lady of Grace," a noble and realistic charter, adapted to the modest needs of their tough trade.

To desire a society in conformity with natural law is a consequence of the interior life. Indeed, the man who has received the truth of Christ, allows Him to purify and convert his soul, and thence becomes fully of the Church—in short, a man who accepts the interior kingship of Jesus cannot set his hand to worldly tasks as though he did not belong to Christ. Whether as father of a family, business leader, poet, or physician, he will seek, in the discharge of his earthly duties, to pay homage to Jesus Christ who dwells in him and is his King and his all. How will he render this homage, and how will he show that he acknowledges Him as King even in his worldly activities? By praying at the beginning of his activities and offering them to God? Certainly. But his activities have their own law. The activities of a physician, a poet, a father of a family, or a business leader must be upright; they are governed by a certain natural law. Therefore it is by fulfilling these earthly tasks in accordance with natural law, and not merely putting them within a religious framework, that the Christian manifests the kingship of Christ in his secular activities.

So far, I have considered the Christian individually. In reality, things are not so simple. Man is not a windowless, doorless monad; a Christian lives in society. Hence, the interior reign of Jesus Christ demands not only that personal activities be performed in religion, love, and conformity with natural law, but also that morals, customs, and laws conform to that same law.

If the reign of Christ is interior and ecclesial, it inevitably follows that it is social, not in the sense that Christ wields political authority Himself or through instituted ministers, nor in the sense that he establishes the laws and customs of temporal societies, but in the sense that His interior or ecclesial kingship guides secular activities in the direction of fidelity to divine law, and tends to give certain form to laws and customs. It forbids some, and develops others.

I hasten to conclude with a quotation and commentary from an oft-cited passage from the encyclical *Quas primas*: "Nor is there any difference in this matter [the universality of Christ's Empire] between the individual and the family or the State; for men are no less subject to the authority of Christ in their collective life than in their private lives." *No less*, because Christ's law and the action of His grace reach men in their collective life as well as their private lives. No less, but *in another way*. It is quite evident, to take an example, that if Christ's law and the influence of His grace should touch the intimate depths of a painter's or an architect's heart and awaken them to a life of prayer and union with God, the life-giving and transformative power of Christ would neither teach them the rules of their craft nor dictate the wisest path within their profession. The spiritual action of Christ and His Church would influence the structure of their profession, shaping it in accordance with justice (taking account of the concrete historical context). Yet Christ's purifying work upon the creative imagination would enable their art to bear its richest fruit. It would not directly change their creative imagination. When it comes to collective life—politics, culture, and civilization—Christ's authority assumes a form distinct from that in private life, in the interior realm, the secret of the heart, and communion with God within the Church. This is why the Lord steadfastly refused to be a king like the rulers of this world. It is sometimes said that His kingship is not of this world, but over this world. This is quite true, but one must understand that this kingship over matters of this world, such as technology, culture, and government, is not the same as His kingship over the Church, nor His reign in the order of conversion and the life of grace.

What, then, are the characteristics of Jesus Christ's kingship over things of this world, and how is it realized? First, Christ sanctifies men deeply enough that they fulfil with holiness—and therefore by doing all that is just—the various duties of their life in this world: in family, profession, and government. Next, Christ, through His Church, safeguards and explains natural law, a Christian natural law. The Church, Bride of Christ, not only proclaims Revelation, but also declares the natural law, so that families, professions, and the State may act with Christian justice, promoting both human welfare and the theological life. Finally, in certain cases, Christ acts through His Church with authority even in matters in themselves temporal, but which have become matters of the Church—spiritual matters *ratione peccati*.[7] Belonging to a union, for instance, is normally a temporal matter, but in particular circumstances, *ratione peccati*, the Church may forbid membership in a given union in the name of Jesus Christ.

Moreover, political history since the first proclamation of the Gospel abundantly shows that Holy Church, which is identical with Jesus' spiritual kingdom, cannot avoid giving rise to and preserving a certain kind of civilization. The Church extends into Christendom precisely insofar as her members participate in civil society, holding offices and responsibilities. I fully acknowledge that the Church transcends civilizations and is not to be equated with any of them. But across different civilizations, the Church, Jesus' spiritual kingdom, endeavours to maintain the enduring standards of natural law, regardless of historical vicissitudes.

One might retort that Our Lord Jesus, in His answer to Pilate, did not make the least allusion to the social consequences of His spiritual kingship. The observation is certainly correct. We should answer, however, that Our Lord's Revelation, as He declared on several occasions,[8] had to be made explicit by His Spouse, the holy and inspired Church, and that, above all, it was necessary to avoid any ambiguity about the truly unique nature of His kingship.

---

[7] The Church's jurisdiction over the city is but one of the aspects of Christ's kingship over the city. The reader who wishes to study further the proper nature of the Church's jurisdiction over the city can refer to the classic work of Charles Cardinal Journet, *La Juridiction de l'Église sur la Cité* (Paris: Desclée de Brouwer, 1931), especially pp. 113, 114, and 123–136. See also, by the same author, *The Church of the Word Incarnate*, trans. Matthew K. Minerd, vol. 2, *The Internal Structure of the Church* (Steubenville, Ohio: Emmaus Academic, 2025), 162–178.

[8] Parables of the mustard seed and the leaven, and the discourse after the Last Supper, John 16:12.

Once its religious and holy character is recognized, the social consequences naturally follow.

It is evident that secularism cannot claim even the least support from Jesus' answer to Pontius Pilate in the Gospel read at the Mass of Christ the King. Any theory that treats secular affairs and the matters of Caesar as alien to the Lord's spiritual kingdom, doctrine, and grace (to the Church, its mystical fulfilment, which hands on His doctrine and communicates His grace), any theory that would secularize the city, cannot in any way, nor through any serious interpretation, be derived from the Gospel.

Perhaps one objects: "You are looking too far afield, in regions too mystical for something as simple as the normal and honest order of institutions. Why go back to the Gospels and the mysteries of supernatural life? You want an upright society? Well then! This uprightness is a matter of observation, reflection, and common sense. You are free to resort to revelation and mysticism, but perhaps it is not necessary." I understand the objection; I especially understand that it does not take into account the concrete state of our nature. The objection fails to recognize the existential position of our nature, its actual state, what is right for it, and what constitutes its natural law. For our nature and its natural law are in fact in a state of fall and redemption. We are wounded in Adam and redeemed in Jesus Christ.

This is why, if a man rejects the interior reign of Jesus Christ, he will either fail in his labours altogether, or he will work in ways that subvert the establishment and maintenance of a proper and honest civic order. To imagine otherwise would be to misunderstand man—his lamentable tendency to perceive and act wrongly both in his private life and in public—and to forget that the devil is constantly at work, undermining, corroding, and corrupting every honest institution. Without the grace of Christ, we cannot refrain from meeting evil with evil; without the desire for holiness in our thoughts and deeds, sooner or later we will take up the weapons of folly and iniquity in the service of institutions of reason and justice—and in doing so, we will work toward their ruin.

We have explained this at length above. "One must beware of saying that institutions alone are enough, that because the civic order is political in nature, good institutions are sufficient to secure it. After all, institutions are made by men—sinful yet redeemed men—who, through both their failings and their virtues, infinitely surpass the political order and its structures. Men participating in political life are by no means confined to it. That is why it is not enough to say: political effect, political cause. We need to add: political effect, political and superpolitical cause. Political effects in conformity to natural law need Christian heroism and just institutions."[9]

Let history shed light on this. Recall what we have read about the Hundred Years' War, the reign of Charles VI, and the early years of Charles VII. We see plainly that political outcomes— the independence of a kingdom, the end of factional strife, or the recognition of the legitimate sovereign before God and for God's sake—were achieved solely through the Maid's sanctity and could not have been secured by other means. Wisdom and generosity that did not flow from union with Jesus Christ would have been futile and powerless.[10]

Furthermore, in our present condition, even purely political outcomes involve men and a city that are no

---

[9] *Sur nos routes d'exil, les Béatitudes*, 153.
[10] On this matter, see, for instance, the works by Olivier Leroy on Joan of Arc, or the excellent little book by Régine Pernoud, *Joan of Arc: Her Story*, trans. Jeremy duQuesnay Adams (New York: St. Martin's Griffin, 1998).

longer in their natural state but exist within a Christian framework. Or, from another perspective, natural law properly formulates the inherent laws of human beings and earthly society, yet these laws can be practiced—and even fully understood—only in a Christian order. This is why I usually speak of "natural law within a Christian order," or "natural law open to the Gospel." In our actual situation, natural law is not closed; it cannot be. It is the law of a nature that is not closed but is corrupted by the devil and given life by the grace of the redemptive Cross. Under these circumstances, how can we hope to implement a natural law open to the Gospel, a natural law within a Christian order, if we remain closed to the Gospel, refusing to allow Jesus Christ to reign freely over our soul, mind, heart, and all our strength? Consider marriage and the family, children's education, working conditions, and the role of money. How can institutions that are not open to the Gospel properly order family, educational, professional, and economic realities? Common sense can fully perceive them only if guided by Christian sense. Good will shall succeed in establishing sound customs only if purified and strengthened by the grace of Jesus Christ.

From all of this, the implications are clear. While Christ's reign in the religious sphere—in the order of conversion and the life of grace—is carried out primarily through the priesthood, for the priest is the minister of grace and the Gospel, Christ's reign over the things of this world is exercised primarily through the laity. It is the special duty of laymen to promote and sustain temporal institutions that reflect Christian justice.

In this difficult work that always has to be undertaken anew, they must not let themselves be misled by the temptation of secularism. Yet they should also firmly push back against meddling clerics and all kinds of clericalism,[11] including that backwards clericalism we see spreading today, where priests invoke religion and the Gospel to turn laymen off from building a temporal order in line with religion and the Gospel.

Still, clergymen's betrayals do not abolish the clerical office. With her priests and hierarchy, the Church will always remain the intelligent and faithful Spouse, incapable of altering the word of her Lord. With infallible certainty, the Church proclaims and interprets the Gospel message for each new generation: the Beatitudes, purification of heart, worship in spirit and truth, the primacy of contemplation. Clergymen's faults should not prevent laymen from heeding this message, which, in fact, the clerics themselves should be the first to hear. Laymen, in order to advance the social kingship of Christ within the social order, must listen to the Church's teaching on the social Christian order, *but first to her instruction on the Christian religious order*. They must see the link between the two. Indeed, the link already exists, so they must reflect upon it carefully.

If they heed the voice of the Spouse, they will learn to employ only pure means. And this is of vital importance. For the Christian social order is an order of truth and justice, how could one serve it, how could one work within it without hypocrisy, were one not carefully to use only the

---

[11] On clerics' encroachments and abuses, it is worth revisiting an old text by Maritain, still relevant thirty years later: "We acknowledge and appreciate the generous intentions of the author . . . but we also feel compelled to point out that religious, happily cut off by their three vows from the tempests of the world, have something better to do than *Platonize about Eros*. The less-protected life of the layman, struggling in this vale of tears, at least *assures him of a much more reliable experience on certain subjects*" (*The Degrees of Knowledge*, 283n).

weapons of truth and justice? Yet such weapons cannot be wielded, nor even recognized, without an ardent desire for purity of heart and prayer that gradually permeates the entire realm of the affections. "Seek ye first the Kingdom of God and His justice."[12] Purity of means, the genuine primacy of contemplation, and a realistic effort to foster or defend honest institutions are intimately connected.

In the necessary struggle to bring social and political life back to Jesus Christ, laymen must not let themselves be pulled away from interior things. They need to know that working to reform institutions in this world would fall far short if we did not wish to be purified ourselves, and purified through that very work in the world. Finally, they must understand that there is a way to go about this temporal work that actually deepens the purification of the heart and deepens prayer.

The Christian temporal order—that is, Christian civilization in its diverse forms throughout history—can never achieve the same purity as the Christian spiritual order, that is, Holy Church. While the Church calls her children to be fully her own and to be perfect as the heavenly Father is perfect,[13] and provides them with the means to attain this holiness, a fatherland, even a Christian one, or a professional association, even a Christian one, cannot, by their very nature, require holiness. Unlike the Church, a fatherland or professional association does not exist at the level of communion with God and redeeming grace. The reign of Christ over temporal affairs, even at its most splendid, can never match the spotless beauty of His reign over the spiritual; only the holy city is completely beautiful.[14]

---

[12] Matthew 6:33.
[13] Matthew 5:48.
[14] Ephesians 5:27.

The Christian temporal order is imperfect in its degree
of purity, and it is imperfect for another reason too. It is
always under attack and persecution from without, while
Pharisaism tries to undermine it from within.

Should we then give up on establishing or preserving
a Christian temporal order? God forbid. We have shown
at length that institutions must be made worthy of Jesus
Christ in order to support His interior reign in souls and
His ecclesial reign. Even though Christian civilization, in
its various historical forms, shall perforce remain imperfect, our commitment to it is not imperfect. We shall fight
with all our heart, employing pure and proper arms.[15] A
Christian's efforts in the temporal realm are like a mother
tending her sick child. Even knowing that the child's
health, if restored, might remain fragile and threatened,
the mother does not care for him half-heartedly. Her love
for her child, together with her fidelity to God, calls for
her entire devotion. Her maternal care, calm and composed, imbued with peace and trust, is nonetheless complete and total.

---

[15] We have often spoken of the infallible and ceaseless victory of
the Church of Jesus Christ and shown that, by virtue of this victory,
at least a minimal portion of the Christian temporal order shall
always survive. The Christian's spiritual kingdom—the Church—
shall always keep alive some part of Christian civilization, however
small. From a human perspective, we could characterize Christ's
kingship as the spontaneous and overflowing submission of our soul
and activity to the light and sanctifying action of the Son of God
our Saviour, through the theological virtues within the Church. It
is He Himself who gives us theological life in and through His
Church, and this theological life, by its very nature, makes its influence felt on all our activities, whether relating to the things of God
or the things of Caesar.

Our Lady in the
Times of Antichrist

"**I** SHOULD LIKE TO LIVE IN THE TIME
of Antichrist,"[1] wrote little Thérèse on her death-
bed. There can be no doubt that the Carmelite, who
offered herself as *a holocaust to merciful love*, shall intercede especially when Antichrist appears. There can be no
doubt that she already prays in a particular way for our
own age, when the precursors of Antichrist have infiltrated
the Church. Above all, her prayer merges into a supplication that is, as it were, infinitely more powerful, that of the
Virgin Mother of God. She crushes the Dragon through
her Immaculate Conception and virginal motherhood, is
glorified even in her body, reigns in heaven alongside her
Son, and presides sovereignly over all the epochs of our
history, especially over those most perilous for souls: the
time of the coming of Antichrist and its preparation by his
diabolical precursors.

Mary manifests herself not only as the powerful and
consoling Virgin in times of distress for the earthly city

---

[1] To be precise, "I should like that those torments [the lot of Christians at time of Antichrist] be reserved to me" (Letter to Sœur Marie
du Sacré-Cœur, in *Manuscrits autiobiographiques*).

and bodily life. She shows herself above all as the helping Virgin, *strong as an army in battle array*, in times when Holy Church is laid waste and her children suffer spiritual agony. She is queen for all of human history, *not only in times of distress but in apocalyptic times as well.*

The Great War was a time of distress: badly prepared offensives leading to slaughter, soldiers crushed under a hurricane of iron and fire: Rossignol Forest and Caures Wood, Death Ravine and the Chemin des Dames.... How many men, buckling on their belts, set out with the terrible certainty that they would perish in that nightmarish whirlwind, never to see victory? Sometimes, and most cruelly, doubt crept into their minds about the worth of their leaders and the soundness of their command. But on one point they had no doubt, on a question that trumped all others: that of spiritual authority.

The chaplain who ministered to these men, called to serve their fatherland unto death, was unshakably firm about every article of faith. It would never have occurred to him to invent some kind of "pastoral" alteration of the holy Mass. He celebrated the holy Sacrifice according to the ancient rite and words, with devotion all the deeper and supplication all the more fervent, knowing that at any moment he, an unarmed priest, and his armed parishioners might be called to unite their own sacrifices, as poor redeemed sinners, to the one Sacrifice of the "Son of God who takes away the sins of the world." The chaplain's fidelity rested calmly on the fidelity of the Church hierarchy, which guarded and defended Christian doctrine and traditional worship, and which did not hesitate to exclude heretics and traitors from Catholic communion. On the battlefield, soon, perhaps in just a few minutes, bodies would be torn apart in unspeakable horror, perhaps slowly asphyxiated under clouds of gas. Yet despite the agony of the body, the soul would remain intact, its serenity unaltered, its deepest refuge unthreatened. Not even the darkest demon, the prince of lies, could raise its mocking laugh. The soul would not fall prey to the treacherous, cowardly attacks of the pseudo-prophets of a pseudo-Church. Even amidst bodily torment, the soul would soar from the quiet shelter of protected faith towards the radiant refuge of the beatific vision in Paradise.

The Great War was a time of distress. We have now entered a time of Apocalypse. Undoubtedly, we are not yet facing the hurricane of fire that ravages the body, but we are already witnessing the agony of souls, because spiritual authority no longer seems concerned with defending them. It appears indifferent both to the truth of doctrine and to the integrity of worship, *having conspicuously abandoned the task of condemning the guilty.* This is the agony of souls within Holy Church, corroded from within by traitors and heretics who have still not been excommunicated. Throughout history, there have already been other times of Apocalypse. Recall, for example, the interrogations of Joan of Arc, deprived of the sacraments by churchmen and confined in the depths of her dark cell under the guard of frightful gaolers. Yet the times of Apocalypse are always marked by the victories of grace. For even when the beasts of the Apocalypse enter the holy city and expose it to the utmost perils, the Church does not cease to be the Church: the beloved city, impregnable to the devil and his minions, pure and without blemish, over which Our Lady reigns as queen.

She, the Immaculate Queen, shall have Christ her Son cut short the dark years of Antichrist. Even then—especially then—she shall win for us the grace to persevere and grow in holiness. She shall preserve for us the share of legitimate spiritual authority we absolutely need. Her presence at Calvary, standing at the foot of the Cross, gives us infallible assurance of this. She stood at the foot of the Cross of her Son, the Son of God in person, to unite herself more perfectly to His redemptive sacrifice and merit in Him every grace for the children of adoption. Every grace: the grace to face the temptations and trials that mark even the most united lives, but also the grace to persevere, rise again, and grow holy amidst the worst ordeals: the trials of bodily exhaustion and the far darker trials of the soul's agony, the trials when the earthly city becomes prey to invaders, and especially when the Church of Jesus Christ must resist self-destruction. By standing at the foot of her Son's Cross, this Virgin Mother whose soul was pierced by a sword of sorrow, this divine Virgin who was crushed and overwhelmed as no creature ever will be, shows us beyond any doubt that she shall be able to sustain the redeemed during the most unimaginable trials, with an intercession that is both completely pure and all-powerful in its motherly care. This most gentle Virgin, Queen of martyrs, persuades us that victory is hidden in the Cross itself and shall be manifested: the bright morning of resurrection will soon dawn for the day without end of the Church triumphant.

In Jesus' Church, beset by modernism even among its leaders at every level of the hierarchy, the suffering of souls and the sting of scandal reach a harrowing intensity. It is an unprecedented drama. Yet the grace of the Son of God, the Redeemer, runs deeper than this drama. And the intercession of the Immaculate Heart of Mary, which obtains all grace, never ceases. In the most downcast souls, those closest to giving up, the Virgin Mary intervenes day and night to unravel this drama in a mysterious way, mysteriously shattering the chains that demons thought unbreakable. *Solve vincla reis.*

Let all of us whom the Lord Jesus Christ, by a singular mark of honor, calls to faithfulness in these new perils— a struggle unlike anything we have known, the struggle against the precursors of Antichrist who have infiltrated the Church—turn back to our hearts and our faith. Let us remember that we believe in the divinity of Jesus and the divine and spiritual motherhood of Mary Immaculate. Let us at least glimpse the fulness of grace and wisdom hidden in the Heart of the Son of God made man, which flows effectively to all who believe. Let us also glimpse the fulness of tenderness and intercession that is the unique privilege of the Immaculate Heart of the Virgin Mary. Let us turn to Our Lady as her children. We will then know, in a way beyond words, that the times of Antichrist are in fact the times of victory, the victory of the complete Redemption of Jesus Christ and the sovereign intercession of Mary.

FATHER ROGER-THOMAS CALMEL, a priest of the Order of Friars Preacher, was born on 11 May 1914, baptized two days later in Sauveterre-la-Lémance (Lot-et-Garonne), and died on 3 May 1975. He was buried on 5 May, the feast of the Dominican pope Saint Pius V, in the garden of the teaching Dominicans of the Immaculate Heart of Saint-Pré, in Brignoles (Var), where one can venerate his tomb.

He came to *Itinéraires* in 1958. We worked together for seventeen years. His contract was expressed in few words: I had asked him to be, at the review, a priest of the Order of Saint Dominic. He replied that he could not and would not be anything else.

But in 1958, we did not yet imagine where this would lead us.

Yet already there were difficulties. They may appear harmless to us now, compared with what came later. Harmless perhaps, but of the same nature as those of today. They were no ordinary difficulties. The Church was increasingly occupied by an enemy faction, a power alien to her historic being. The Church of France at least, despite Pius XII and a Roman Curia that still counted Ottaviani and Pizzardo among its members, was held and lorded over by a Masonic and modernist Left, crowned by the cardinalatial trio of Liénart, Feltin, and Gerlier. Dominicans spoke, wrote, and published everywhere, so long as it was for the Left and to the Left, always sheltered by their local superiors. But that Father Calmel should intend to write in *Itinéraires* was, in France, already in 1958, still under Pius XII, an intolerable scandal. It was not possible, it was not permitted.

Later on, Dominicans of the Chenu–Congar faction
liked to say that they had been martyred under Pius XII.
They were very little, in truth, for despite a few Roman
sanctions their faction remained dominant in France,
where it harassed and persecuted at will those Dominicans accused of "integrism," preventing them from writ-
ing and speaking. Thus the first articles of Father Calmel
in *Itinéraires* had to appear under the pseudonym "Roger
Thomas." I had to go all the way to Rome to obtain permission from the highest level of the Dominican Order's
government and from the Roman Curia. It was only
in May 1959 that he was able at last to sign his own
name. John XXIII had barely settled in, and Rome con-
soled itself by whispering: "The popes pass, the Curia
remains." An axiom often confirmed in the past, but
which was soon to be overturned, though not so long as
Cardinal Tardini still lived. At the beginning of 1959, it
was still possible to be heard in Rome, and the authori-
zation granted to Father Calmel to write as much as he
wished in *Itinéraires* came from so high a source that no
one, for a long time, dared call it into question—until the
day when such authorizations, having lost all moral force,
were simply ignored.

At the time of Pius XII, the dominant faction in the
Church of France regularly accused us of papolatry. The
charge was unfair, because we were not idolaters, but
we were over the top and imprudent. We had entirely
forgotten the condemnation of Action Française, because
we were fortunate enough to have a Pius XII! We really
were fortunate, and we knew it too. Marcel Clément's
ardent preaching, so felicitously insightful and eloquent
in expounding the reigning pope's doctrine, kept us attentive to this good fortune. But even then, he was already
showing a tendency towards indiscriminate loyalty, with

an enthusiasm that disregarded the nuances, careful distinctions, and limits that the Church had always upheld in her teachings on obedience.

But there were two writers in *Itinéraires* who never had anything to do with these Clementino-Papist exaggerations: Louis Salleron and Father Calmel. They scarcely knew each other, yet each in his own way resisted that spirit. Louis Salleron used to warn us, "You will get a nasty shock when one day you have two or three popes at once...." We brushed him off, saying that such things did not happen every day. Well, what we got with Paul VI was worse. For the two or three popes who fought over Peter's throne back in the day all shared, at least, the same religion, the same Mass, and the same catechism. With Paul VI, the pope himself no longer had the Mass of the pope. The pope had separated himself from himself. He abandoned the Mass of his ordination and tried to ban the Mass he had celebrated during the first years of his pontificate. At the time of Pius XII, we never imagined the possibility of such an abomination.

Marcel Clément, following Jean Ousset, kept quoting Saint Pius X: "There can be no holiness where there is dissent from the pope." Father Calmel fought hard against this idea. The authority invoked did not faze him. Certainly, Saint Pius X is Saint Pius X; Father Calmel revered him completely, but this was a private opinion, and one that was mistaken. The history of the Church shows us canonized saints who openly disagreed with popes who have not been canonized. Father Calmel also had recourse to theology, as well as plain common sense. In that same address to priests on 2 December 1912, so often reprinted in all those editions of *Pour qu'il règne* (p. 492, note 9), Saint Pius X declared, "One cannot limit the sphere in which the pope can and must exercise his will." If one takes this to mean that there are no limits at all, or only whatever limit each pope feels like recognizing, with no objective standard, then one falls into an obvious error, Father Calmel used to tell us. But he spoke in vain. We failed to see the error. We had Pius XII.

Subsequent events soon set us straight.

Those who met Father Calmel after reading his work were struck to discover a man whose slight frame seemed so disproportionate to his moral authority. Physically he was frail, sickly-looking, and actually sick quite often. All his life he had been burdened by a congenital weakness of the heart. I think Pascal, whom he loved (whom he canonized), helped him in living with the persistent pain of bodily weakness and suffering. But what a soul in that ailing, feeble body. The soul of a crusader.

Even before the Council, he was heavily persecuted by his fellow Dominicans. The persecution was even physical, mainly through noise, which he could not bear, and deprivation of sleep. Knowing how fragile his health was, they struck at that weakness, to the point where he became deathly ill. He then had to be rescued from the convents of his persecutors by means of medical certificates, and assisted in finding peaceful refuges. But this left him heartbroken: "I became a Dominican," he said, "in order to live in community with brethren." But no Dominican community was brotherly to him anymore. Everywhere he was treated as an enemy, sometimes with malice and hostility, sometimes with polite indifference, but always as an enemy. Against such moral and social persecution, there is no human remedy. He called it "sociological relegation." But he added, "What are the thousand small, daily consequences of this sociological relegation compared to the honour Jesus Christ does us in granting us to confess the faith?"

After the Council ended in December 1965, the French bishops condemned *Itinéraires* in June 1966 for the crime of opposing the new spirit. But from 1966 to 1969, the bishops themselves were more or less uncertain of Rome's true intentions, despite sometimes receiving secret encouragement to subversion. So what did Paul VI want? What did he actually want? In 1967, he proclaimed a "year of faith" aimed—he himself declared—against the "post-Conciliar mentality," which he reproached for having "propagated the vain hope of giving Christianity a new interpretation." In 1968, he brought this "year of faith" to a close by delivering his famous "profession of faith." Later it became clear that everything happened as if Paul VI were not trying to stop the Conciliar evolution, but to allay and thus neutralize the fears that might have slowed it down. At the time, plenty of ecclesiastical hierarchs, not knowing which way the wind was blowing, preferred to play it safe and bide their time, protecting their careers while everything went to pieces.

At least Father Calmel got some breathing room out of it. With all the confusion, nobody made any serious moves against him. Several times they dropped hints that his permission to write for *Itinéraires* was about to be withdrawn. "Make sure to remind them," I told him, "that there is a third party here. I am the one who asked for this permission; it was granted to me." By some relief that Providence brought to our troubles, there were few, if any, juridical or administrative measures taken against us. Ecclesiastical law retained some moral weight over men's consciences, although it was already beginning to self-destruct. But soon the blow fell: in 1968, the French bishops murdered the Catholic catechism, and in 1969, Rome strangled the traditional Mass. This forced us into a terrible kind of freedom.

Father Calmel's soul remains with us. It is present in his writings, standing on tiptoes, full of the Church's common doctrine and common prayer, stretching upward to grow in God's love. For him theology, liturgy, and the Dominican constitutions were not guides or regulations, but a source of inner nourishment. In our midst he fulfilled his task as a friar preacher, son of Saint Dominic, disciple of Saint Thomas, priest of Jesus Christ, and apostle of the Rosary.

He endures.

Jean Madiran